WHAT HAPPENED TO ME?

WHAT HAPPENED TO ME?

✦

Reflections of a Journey

Randall Niles

iUniverse, Inc.

New York Lincoln Shanghai

WHAT HAPPENED TO ME?
Reflections of a Journey

iUniverse, Inc.

For information address:
iUniverse, Inc.
2021 Pine Lake Road, Suite 100
Lincoln, NE 68512
www.iuniverse.com

First published August 2004.
Cover design and photography by Bryan Cole, Colorado Springs, Colorado.

ISBN: 0-595-32971-3

Printed in the United States of America

To Mom—

Your legacy lives on!

Contents

ACKNOWLEDGMENTS

My heart is forever dedicated to my precious wife, Debra, and my three kids, Griffin, Austin and Lauryn. Thanks for supporting me in these crazy adventures…You guys make it all worthwhile…!

Thanks to my Dad, who's supported me through thick and thin. Thanks for letting me share…Thanks for taking an honest journey with me…

Above all, thanks to my Creator, who graciously woke me from a long, long slumber…

INTRODUCTION

I wrote this book to explain what happened to me…

Until a few years ago, I was a successful businessman and attorney. I had degrees from top universities and I was fairly well-traveled. My family, friends and peers knew me as intellectual, motivated and reasonably balanced. I had a great wife and kids, and I was generally healthy…

I was considered a success by the world's standards.

In what seemed to be overnight, people witnessed a dramatic shift in my life. From their perspective, I hastily left the corporate and legal worlds and started serving full-time in some sort of "religious" group. Without pay, I gave tirelessly of my time and resources. I started writing books and speaking at outreach events. To my family, friends and peers, I was immersed in the kind of "religious movement" that I had so passionately rejected most of my life.

What happened?

Was I somehow brainwashed to become a sort of religious fanatic?

Was I reacting to my mom's death by grasping for some kind of supernatural crutch?

Had the logical atheist really bought into a narrow-minded mythology story?

◆   ◆   ◆

I wrote this book to explain what happened to me…

SOME BACKGROUND

I was raised in a Bible-believing home by a loving Christian mother. However, by the end of 7th grade, I labeled myself a "hypocrite" and stopped attending church. By the end of high school, I called myself an "agnostic" and was totally removed from "spiritual" things. By the time I graduated from college, I had converted to "atheism," because I believed that maintaining an agnostic label was itself hypocritical. By the time I graduated from law school, I was a "practicing atheist," operating in accordance with my own intellectual brand of materialism, naturalism and moral relativism.

So, what happened?

I think I've isolated three primary reasons why I rejected my childhood "religion" so dramatically:

Youthful Skepticism

When I was about eleven-years-old, I started asking questions about everything, including God, the Bible, and the "meaning of life" in general. Unequipped to deliver any kind of foundational evidence, my church and family relied on the axiom, "you've just got to have faith."

That didn't work for me…

20th Century Science

During high school, I started absorbing the latest scientific discoveries and technological advances. I bought into the notion that 20th century technology finally explained everything. Since naturalistic science was taught as "fact", I saw the Christian worldview as "silly" and "wishful thinking."

There wasn't much need for God anymore…

Intellectual Worldview

During college, I started expanding my horizons by taking theology, philosophy, sociology, and history courses. I used the opportunity to create my very own worldview—a kind of "socio-philosophical-intellectual brand of religion."

I was very secure in my humanist belief system…

So, there you have it. I spent the next couple of decades focusing on personal achievement and material success. I studied business, finance and law at schools like Georgetown, Oxford and Berkeley. I worked in glass-towered law firms and high-flying technology companies. To me, life was about self and success. Since completing high school biology and college philosophy, I could care less about "metaphysical" things. I was done with that phase of my life—I wasn't even asking the basic questions any more: "Where did I come from?" "Why am I here?" or "Where am I going when I die?" It just didn't matter to me...

Based on my intellect and experience, I created my own worldview—my own philosophy for living. Using standard cultural labels, I guess I was a materialist, naturalist, relativist, humanist, hedonist that had it pretty well together. Truly, I felt successful and happy. I didn't need a supernatural reason for anything. Metaphysical thought was for philosophers and theologians. "Religion" was OK for those who needed a crutch to limp through a difficult life—as long as they didn't limp in my direction.

I based my daily conduct on a "social contract" view of the world—it just made sense to treat others well, maintain ethics in business, and lovingly support my family. Those of us with resources and opportunities somehow had a social obligation to "give back" to our community. This was a rational view of the world, and I didn't need any kind of supernatural notion of "absolute truth" or morality to adhere to these common sense principles.

I marched to this drum for nearly 20 years...

◆   ◆   ◆

On October 5, 1999, my comfortable worldview took a mighty blow...

Mom had just endured another round of chemotherapy, and she was scheduled to get her test results. She called and asked if I would attend the visit with her oncologist. Of course, I agreed to take a morning off work to help Mom "collect information."

As I sat in the doctor's office and listened to the medical report, the bottom of my stomach dropped to the floor. My secure worldview was sliced through in an instant—my presuppositions about life, death, purpose, and meaning started peeling away like an onion…I listened as we were told about "elevated cancer markers" and a "diminishing list of treatment alternatives." I was truly staggered…I was just trying to maintain my emotional bearings…

Then reality hit…

The reality of the disease, the reality of the prognosis, the reality that this was my precious Mom enduring real pain, the reality of life, and the reality of death. All of a sudden, I felt very awkward and alone. I was shocked by the truth of my mom's disease. Even more powerfully, I was appalled at my total apathy towards discovering truth, purpose and meaning to that point in my life. It was then and there that I realized I needed to do more than mask feelings with rationalist dribble.

Dying hadn't really been in my vocabulary up until then, at least not in such a personal way. Sure, I knew death was inevitable—but it was way out there somewhere and I didn't need to think about it yet. Suddenly, I did need to think about it. What did it all mean? What was it all about?

I was emotionally invested…As part of that investment, I started thinking again. I started asking questions again. I started challenging my worldview from different perspectives. I truly started an open and honest journey for truth…

◆   ◆   ◆

Mom died on April 30, 2002. To many, Mom's battle with cancer and ultimate death clouded my rational view of the world and opened me up to some sort of emotion-based "religious experience." The purpose of this book is to explain that I'm more rational, logical and intellectual than ever. I just used this season of trial in my life to dig in, open my eyes, and discover some stunning things in our world.

It's from this basis that I want to share some of my journey with you…

PART I

THE COMPLEXITY OF LIFE

MY PRIOR WORLDVIEW

Naturalistic Presuppositions

My biggest barrier to any kind of religious faith was 20th century science and technology. To me, supernatural faith was merely a product of simple, ancient peoples trying to explain the world around them—the sun, the moon and the stars; seasonal crop cycles; human reproduction, etc.

Well, those ancient days are gone. We now understand the world around us—we've mapped the cosmos, we've mastered agrarian techniques, and we've deciphered the human genome. In a nutshell, 20th century advances in science and technology removed the need for God (any kind of a god).

More specifically, here's what I believed...

All things—from the massive cosmos to the microscopic cell—are the result of unguided natural processes over millions and billions of years. Everything is explained by the physical—there's no need for any notion of the metaphysical. Everything is the result of wonderful chance, held together by chemical-based systems, natural laws and properties of physics. Smart people with telescopes and microscopes "broke the code" once and for all using 20th century technology. The "facts" of science trump anything philosophical or religious. Done.

Maybe the introduction to the Emmy-award-winning PBS NOVA special on evolution called "The Miracle of Life" summed up my views best...

> Four and half billion years ago, the young planet Earth was a mass of cosmic dust and particles. It was almost completely engulfed by the shallow primordial seas. Powerful winds gathered random molecules from the atmosphere. Some were deposited in the seas. Tides and currents swept the molecules together. And somewhere in this ancient ocean the miracle of life began... The first organized form of primitive life was a tiny protozoan. Millions of protozoa populated the ancient seas. These early organisms were completely self-sufficient in their sea-water world. They moved about their aquatic environment feeding on bacteria and other organisms... From these one-celled organisms evolved all life on earth.[1]

---

1.   NOVA, "The Miracle of Life," WGBH Educational Foundation, 1986 (Swedish Television Corp., 1982), videotape.

A Simple Thought

Sometimes it takes a simple thought to shake the foundation of an entire thought system...

It was during a youth sports camp in late 1999 that I had an effortless epiphany.

"Make sure your kids drink plenty of water," we were told. "Hydration, hydration, hydration—that's the key."

"No problem," I thought. "Everyone knows this basic principle of *nutritional science.*"

Then it hit me...

When I was playing sports as a kid, water was treated merely as a reward. Even if we got a moment at the drinking fountain, the coaches would monitor our time so we didn't drink too much. "You'll get a stitch in your side!" they said. In fact, at half time, we only got orange slices, because fluids would "cramp us up and slow us down."

Then, I remembered my father's experience with sports as a kid. During his generation, athletes actually took salt tablets—sometimes in large amounts. Coaches actually viewed hydration during a game as taboo.

Ka-zip (or whatever it sounds like when a shutter clicks on a camera)! I had one of those "picture-moment" experiences, where a truth comes into focus and sticks with you forever...

Science isn't static. Science changes over time. The observable evidence doesn't change, but the scientific understanding of that evidence does...

In my straightforward illustration, three generations of athletes faced three different views of nutritional science. The observable evidence regarding water and the human body didn't change, but the scientific presentation (and especially, the public perception) of that evidence advanced at least three times over a few decades.

For some reason, this simple thought challenged me.

For some reason, this inconsequential moment in my life opened a floodgate of far-reaching questions.

I needed to look at the observable evidence again. It was time to start examining my decades-old presuppositions about science, nature and technology. I decided to go back to the big picture basics of the world around me...I started to read and study...

WHAT I DISCOVERED

How Do Scientists Currently Explain the Origin of the Universe?

It seems the Big Bang Theory and its related Inflation Universe Theories (IUTs) are still today's dominant scientific conjectures about the origin of the universe. According to these interrelated notions, the universe was created between 13 and 20 billion years ago from the random, cosmic explosion of a subatomic ball that hurled space, time, matter and energy in all directions. Everything—the whole universe—came from an initial speck of infinite density (also known as a "singularity"). This speck (existing outside of space and time) appeared from no where, for no reason, only to explode all of a sudden. Over a period of approximately 10 billion years, this newly created space, time, matter and energy evolved into remarkably-designed and fully-functional stars, galaxies and planets, including our earth.

Sounds familiar...I'll move on...

How Do Scientists Currently Explain the Origin of Life?

Generally, evolutionary theory is still the foundation of today's scientific worldview. By and large, the text books teach that organic life sprung from non-organic matter exclusively through a natural mechanistic process on a pre-biotic earth. That original life form then evolved into more complex life forms through a natural process of random mutations and natural selection. In a nutshell, the majority scientific hypothesis is that matter randomly acting on matter for a long period of time created everything we see.

That's pretty much what I remember—no real change there...

Wait! My skeptical mind started churning...

How can nothing explode? Where did all that matter and energy come from? What caused its release? How did this explosion of everything (from nothing) order itself? How can simplicity become complexity? Where did the chemical elements come from? Where did the mathematical laws and physical properties come from? How do we explain the design, complexity and fine-tuning inherent in spiral galaxies, solar systems and stars?

How did life come from a rock? How did a bird come from a lizard? Why don't we see birds come from lizards today? Why are there no transitional fossils in our museums today? Why have we never observed beneficial mutations? Where did the information code in DNA come from? Where did the language convention that interprets DNA come from? How can we explain the random development of the human eye, reproductive system, digestive tract, brain, heart and lungs? What about the subconscious mind? What about love, morality, ethics and emotions? Can these things really evolve gradually and randomly over time?

Jeepers! What was happening to me?

Literally, I was in a state of "stream-of-consciousness" skepticism. Everything I knew (and thought I knew) about the world around me didn't make sense any more. I couldn't go back! If I was going to be intellectually honest with myself, I couldn't retreat to my prior way of thinking…I had to go forward and personally look at the observable evidence…But, where to begin?

By chance, a co-worker had collected a few of today's high school biology text books. I opened one on a lark, and was stunned by the first page I saw. There was the same evolutionary chart of species that I remembered from the wall of my high school classroom. It was a tree-like graphic with a bunch of simple life forms at the bottom, and a series of more complex creatures towards the top. I always thought that was a reasonable presentation, but now my skeptical mind was whirring…

Regardless of any theoretical problems with the tree itself, what about all the evolutionary processes required to get to the first simple life forms at the bottom of the chart in the first place?

How Does the Theory of Evolution Really Work?

The evolution tree in my high school classroom only dealt with the macro-evolutionary chain between organic creatures. Through my quick study, I found at least five other fundamental stages of evolution that would be required prior to any possibility of organic life. In fact, each stage seemed essential to the next in the overall theory…

The first is "**Cosmic Evolution**"—the idea that space, time, matter and energy somehow "exploded" (or expanded) from essentially nothing in the sudden "big bang" that was the birth of our universe. The second stage is "**Stellar Evolution**." Since the big bang is thought to have produced only Hydrogen, Helium and a variety of subatomic particles, these elements must have somehow condensed into stars through some sort of evolutionary process. The third stage is "**Chemical Evolution**." According to general thought, the only chemical elements produced by the Big Bang were Hydrogen and Helium (and possibly Lithium). As a result of the incredible heat and pressure within stars, these original elements somehow evolved into the other 88 naturally occurring chemical elements we observe today.

The fourth stage is "**Planetary Evolution**." The complex chemical elements thought to have evolved within ancient stars were somehow ejected, possibly at the violent deaths of stellar life cycles, releasing great clouds of swirling compounds. These clouds of chemical elements somehow formed finely-tuned solar systems, including our own. The fifth phase is "**Organic Evolution**" (also known as "spontaneous generation"). The theory is that the planet Earth began as a molten mass of matter a few billions years ago. It cooled off into solid, dry rock. Then, it rained on the rocks for millions of years, forming great oceans. Eventually, this "prebiotic rock soup" (water + rock) came alive and spawned the first self-replicating organic systems.

OK, now I had more questions than ever, but at least I made it to the base of the so-called evolution tree. This is where the sixth phase of general evolutionary theory occurs—"**Macro Evolution**." All living creatures are thought to share a common ancestor: a relatively "simple" single-celled organism, which evolved from inorganic matter (so-called, "rock soup"). Essentially, the birds and the bananas, the fishes and the flowers, are all genetically related. Oh, we need to add one more…The seventh and final stage of the theory is "**Micro Evolution**." Micro Evolution is the variation and variety of traits expressed in sexually compatible "kinds" of organisms. Examples include the differences between various kinds of horses, dogs, cats, etc. This "variation within a kind" is what Darwin observed in the mid-1800's, and what we still observe today…

OK, let's recap…

Evolutionary Theory appears to have seven distinct and interrelated phases, set by Science in the following order:

> ***Cosmic Evolution.*** The development of space, time, matter and energy from nothing.
>
> ***Stellar Evolution.*** The development of complex stars from the chaotic first elements.
>
> ***Chemical Evolution.*** The development of all chemical elements from an original two.
>
> ***Planetary Evolution.*** The development of planetary systems from swirling elements.
>
> ***Organic Evolution.*** The development of organic life from inorganic matter (a rock).
>
> ***Macro-Evolution.*** The development of one kind of life from a totally different kind of life.
>
> ***Micro-Evolution.*** The development of variations within the same kind of life.

Interestingly, the science books and the television documentaries declare that only the 7th phase—Micro-Evolution—has been observed and documented. The first six phases of evolution are merely assumed…But that's OK, isn't it logical to use Micro-Evolutionary observations to connect the dots on all the other required phases of evolution?

Wait. Where did this come from in the first place? Did this really all start with Darwin? Is this all in Darwin's book? Did I even read that book? It seems everyone remembers reading Darwin's *Origin of Species*, but how many of us really have? Darwinian evolution was presented as such an established fact in my high school biology class, I guess there wasn't any reason to go back and read the original theoretical treatise…

That was then—this is now. I decided to read Darwin's book for myself…

Charles Darwin and his *Origin of Species*

In 1831, Charles Darwin sailed as a passenger on the *HMS Beagle*. His five-year voyage took him to the coasts of South America, where he observed various kinds of animals. One set of creatures in particular, the Galapagos finches, caught Darwin's attention. He studied the birds, collected samples, and observed that they had various beak sizes and shapes. These observed variations inspired the initial development of Darwin's "Theory of Origins." He returned to England in 1836.

In 1842, Darwin began drafting *On the Origin of Species by Means of Natural Selection, or the Preservation of Favoured Races in the Struggle for Life* (often referred to simply as *Origin of Species*). His work was heavily influenced by Sir Charles Lyell's *Principles of Geology* (1830) and Thomas Malthus' *An Essay on the Principle of Population* (1798). *Origin of Species* was ultimately published in 1859.

Guess what? I liked Darwin's book. In a nutshell, *Origin of Species* proposes "Natural Selection" as the mechanism by which an original simple-celled organism could have evolved gradually into all species observed today—both plant and animal. Generally, Darwin presents a theory of evolution, which he defines as "descent with modification." It's a fun read, and a compelling hypothesis for the time.

However, 100 years later, scientists realized that Darwin's basic theory needed work—"Natural Selection" is a conservative process, not a means of developing complexity from simplicity. As scientists started understanding the nature of genetics, they were forced to update Darwin's original theory. They proposed that Natural Selection, in conjunction with genetic mutation, allowed for the development of all species from a common ancestor. Although true beneficial mutations have never been observed (scientists only observe harmful, "downward" mutations), this is today's general conjecture regarding evolutionary change.

But what about the "common ancestor" at the bottom of the evolutionary tree?...

Spontaneous Generation and the First Life Form

Darwinian (and neo-Darwinian) evolution only focuses on the mechanism for modification over time between kinds of organisms. Evolutionary theory still doesn't deal with the first organism that arose by chance on our so-called "primitive planet"—this is called "spontaneous generation."

Without outside input, "spontaneous generation" is really the only explanation for the first organisms on Earth. The concept goes way back to Anaximander, a Greek philosopher in the 6th Century BC, who proposed that life arose from mud when exposed to sunlight. Although Darwin's theory focused on the mechanism for evolutionary change between life forms, he also maintained that original life probably arose from a "little pond" where sunlight was acting on organic salts. In the 1920's, scientists Oparin and Haldane updated the basic conjecture of "spontaneous generation" by proclaiming that ultraviolet light acting on a primitive atmosphere of water, ammonia & methane produced a "hot dilute soup" of basic life.

As I continued my reading, I discovered an interesting theme. The general public and educational media seemed fine with these basic theories and conjectures. However, over the last couple of decades, the scientific community has grown increasingly uneasy. Whereas 20th century science and technology somehow removed the philosophical need for anything metaphysical, 21st century science and technology were revealing things that can't be explained through merely assumed physical processes.

> *Considering the way the prebiotic soup is referred to in so many discussions of the origin of life as an already established reality, it comes as something of a shock to realize that there is absolutely no positive evidence for its existence.*[1]

Something wasn't connecting here—scientists across the board (whether atheist, agnostic or theist) were declaring that *spontaneous generation was disproved one hundred years ago!*[2]

---

1.   Michael Denton, *Evolution: A Theory in Crisis*, Adler and Adler, 1985, 261.
2.   George Wald, "The Origin of Life," *Scientific American*, 191:48, May 1954.

In fact, evolutionary scientists themselves started looking at the odds that a free-living, single-celled organism (a bacterium, for example) could result from a chance combining of life building blocks (amino acids, for example). Harold Morowitz, a renowned physicist from Yale University and author of *Origin of Cellular Life* (1993), declared that the odds for any kind of spontaneous generation were one chance in $10^{100,000,000,000}$.[3]

Sir Fred Hoyle, a popular agnostic who wrote *Evolution from Space* (1981), proposed that such odds were one chance in $10^{40,000}$ ("the same as the probability that a tornado sweeping through a junkyard could assemble a 747").[4]

Francis Crick, an atheist and co-discoverer of the DNA structure in 1953, calls life "almost a miracle."[5] He couldn't rationalize the metaphysical implications of his DNA discovery so he devised his "interstellar spores" theory in the 1970s.

By the way, scientists from various disciplines generally set their "Impossibility Standard" at one chance in 10^{50} (1 in a 100,000 billion, billion, billion, billion, billion). Therefore, whether one chance in $10^{100,000,000,000}$ or one chance in $10^{40,000}$, the notion that life somehow rose from non-life has clearly met the scientific standard for statistical impossibility.

I think Harvard University biochemist and Nobel Laureate George Wald shed perfect light on the whole situation when he declared:

> One has to only contemplate the magnitude of this task to concede that the spontaneous generation of a living organism is impossible. Yet we are here—as a result, I believe, of spontaneous generation.[6]

So, what are these scientists discovering?…Why are they declaring such huge odds against their own theories?…Why are they proposing new (and slightly outlandish) conjectures such as DNA spores from alien cultures?…

Let's take a look…

---

3.   Harold Marowitz, *Energy Flow in Biology*, Academic Press, 1968.
4.   Sir Fred Hoyle, *Nature*, vol. 294:105, November 12, 1981.
5.   Francis Crick, *Life Itself—Its Origin and Nature*, Futura, 1982.
6.   George Wald, "The Origin of Life," *Scientific American*, 191:48, May 1954.

DNA and the Impossibility of Information

The DNA molecule is one of the greatest scientific discoveries of all time. First described by James Watson and Francis Crick in 1953[7], DNA is the famous storehouse of genetics that establishes each organism's physical characteristics. It wasn't until mid-2001, that the Human Genome Project and Celera Genomics jointly presented the true nature and complexity of the digital code inherent in DNA. We now understand that there are approximately 35,000 genes in each human DNA molecule, comprised of chemical bases arranged in approximately 3 billion precise sequences. Even the DNA molecule for the single-celled bacterium, *E. coli*, contains enough information to fill an entire set of *Encyclopedia Britannica*.

DNA (deoxyribonucleic acid) is a double-stranded molecule that is twisted into a helix like a spiral staircase. Each strand is comprised of a sugar-phosphate backbone and numerous base chemicals attached in pairs. The four bases that make up the stairs in the spiraling staircase are adenine (A), thymine (T), cytosine (C) and guanine (G). These stairs act as the "letters" in the genetic alphabet, combining into complex sequences to form the words, sentences and paragraphs that act as instructions to guide the formation and functioning of the host cell. Maybe even more appropriately, the A, T, C and G in the genetic code of the DNA molecule can be compared to the "0" and "1" in the binary code of computer software. Like software to a computer, the DNA code is a genetic language that communicates information to the organic cell.

The DNA code, like a floppy disk of binary code, is quite simple in its basic paired structure. However, it's the sequencing and functioning of that code that's enormously complex. Through recent technologies like x-ray crystallography, we now know that the cell is not a "blob of protoplasm", but rather, a microscopic marvel that is more complex than the space shuttle. The cell is very complicated, using vast numbers of phenomenally precise DNA instructions to control its every function.

Although DNA code is remarkably complex, it's the information translation system connected to that code that really baffles science. Like any language, letters and words mean nothing outside the language convention used to give those let-

---

7.   J.D. Watson and F.H.C. Crick, "Structure of Deoxyribose Nucleic Acid," Nature, 171:737 (1953).

ters and words meaning. This is modern information theory at its core. A simple binary example of information theory is the "Midnight Ride of Paul Revere." In that famous story, Mr. Revere asks a friend to put one light in the window of the North Church if the British came by land, and two lights if they came by sea. Without a shared language convention between Paul Revere and his friend, that simple communication effort would mean nothing. Well, take that simple example and multiply by a factor containing hundreds of zeros.

We now know that the DNA molecule is an intricate message system. To claim that DNA arose randomly is to say that information can develop randomly. Many scientists argue that the chemical building blocks of the DNA molecule can be explained by natural material processes over millions of years. However, explaining the material base of a message is completely independent of the information transmitted using those materials. Thus, the chemical building blocks have nothing to do with the origin of the complex message itself.

As a simple illustration, the information content of the clause "nature and design" has nothing to do with the writing material used, whether ink, paint, chalk or crayon. In fact, the clause can be written in binary code, Morse code or smoke signals, but the message remains the same, independent of the medium. There is obviously no relationship between the information and the material base used to transmit it. Some current theories argue that self-organizing properties within the base chemicals themselves created the information in the first DNA molecule. Others argue that external self-organizing forces created the first DNA molecule. However, all of these theories must hold to the illogical conclusion that the material used to transmit the information also produced the information itself. Although I'm not a scientist, logic tells me that the information contained within the genetic code must be entirely independent of the chemical makeup of the DNA molecule.

Does this science stuff make sense? Am I correctly interpreting the awesome complexity of the DNA molecule that we only recently started to understand? It seems to me that anyone who goes out and truly investigates the miracle of the DNA molecule—this incredible micro, digital, error-correcting, redundant, self duplicating, information storage and retrieval system, with its own inherent language convention, that has the potential to develop any organism from raw biological material—has to be equally awe struck!

> *It is astonishing to think that this remarkable piece of machinery, which possesses the ultimate capacity to construct every living thing that ever existed on Earth, from giant redwood to the human brain, can construct all its own components in a matter of minutes and weigh less than 10^{-16} grams. It is of the order of several thousand million million times smaller than the smallest piece of functional machinery ever constructed by man.[8]*

With the discovery, mapping and sequencing of the DNA molecule over the last few decades, we now understand that organic life is based on vastly complex information code, and, like today's most complex software codes, such information cannot be created or interpreted without some kind of "intelligence." For me, truly understanding the scientific reality of the DNA molecule single-handedly defeated my life-long presupposition that life arose from non-life through random materialistic forces. Even with trillions of years, the development of DNA is statistically impossible.

But, hey, let's dig in further…If DNA is the information storehouse that acts as the blueprint for cellular development, what do these functional cells look like? Are they really all that complex?

The Complexity of the "Simple" Cell

Each person begins as a single cell, formed by the joining of the mother's egg and the father's sperm. That single cell contains the digital code to make thousands of other kinds of cells, from fat cells to bone cells—from brain cells to lung cells. There are muscle cells, skin cells, vein cells, capillary cells and blood cells…Ultimately, from that one original cell, the human body will have something like 30 trillion cells conducting an orchestra of different functions.

In the first half of this century, scientists still assumed that the cell was a fairly simple blob of protoplasm. Without electron microscopes and other technology, the cell was treated as a "black box" that mysteriously performed its various functions—an unobservable collection of "gelatin" molecules whose inner workings were unknown.

---

8.   Michael Denton, *Evolution: A Theory in Crisis*, Adler and Adler, 338.

Through the marvels of 21st century technology, scientists now understand the following:

> *Although the tiniest bacterial cells are incredibly small, weighing less than 10^{-12} grams, each is in effect a veritable micro-miniaturized factory containing thousands of exquisitely designed pieces of intricate molecular machinery, made up altogether of one hundred thousand million atoms, far more complicated than any machinery built by man and absolutely without parallel in the non-living world.*[9]

Each microscopic cell is as functionally complex as a small city. When magnified 50,000 times through electron micrographs, we see that a cell is made up of multiple complex structures, each with a different role in the cell's operation. Using the city comparison, here's a simple chart that reveals the awesome intricacy and design of a typical cell:

City		Cell
Workers	=>	**Proteins**
Power Plant	=>	Mitochondria
Roads	=>	Actin fibers, Microtubules
Trucks	=>	Kinesin, Dynein
Factories	=>	Ribosomes
Library	=>	Genome (DNA, RNA)
Recycling Center	=>	Lysosome
Police	=>	Chaperones
Post Office	=>	Golgi Apparatus

As we delve further into the cellular world, technology is revealing black boxes within previous black boxes. As science advances, more of these black boxes are being opened, exposing an "unanticipated Lilliputian world" of enormous complexity that has pushed the theory of evolution to a breaking point.[10]

---

9.   Denton, 250.
10. Michael J. Behe, *Darwin's Black Box: The Biochemical Challenge to Evolution*, Simon & Schuster, 1996, 18.

Wow! That's at the cellular level. If the cell is that complex, what about the simplest organisms made up of these cellular structures? Is there really such a thing as "simple," now that we can view organisms using the latest in microbiological and biochemical technology?

The Miracle of the "Simple" Organism

If the foundation of today's evolutionary thinking is the first, simple, single-celled organism created in prebiotic rock soup, then what is a "simple" single-celled organism? Is there such a thing? Wouldn't any organism—even the first one—have to synthesize fuel, generate energy, reproduce its kind, etc.?

Therefore, what's considered "simple"?

I guess a fertilized human egg at the moment of conception looks like a simple, single-celled blob no bigger than a pinhead. However, we now know that amorphous blob contains information equivalent to 6 billion "chemical letters"—enough complex code to fill 1,000 books, 500 pages thick with print so small that it would take a microscope to read it.[11] Through the marvel of DNA, every single human trait is established at the moment of conception. Within hours, that single cell starts reproducing and grows a cilia propulsion system to move the fertilized egg (now called a "zygote") towards the uterus. Within six days, the original cell (now called an "embryo") has reproduced its library of information over 100 times. Ultimately, that original blob of gelatin will divide into the 30 trillion cells that make up the human body. At that point, if all the DNA chemical "letters" were printed in books, it's estimated those books would fill the Grand Canyon—fifty times![12]

OK, I don't see anything "simple" there...

But that's a human egg, not a simple, self-existing, biological entity. Let's get back on track and look at a simple organism that exists in nature...

How about a "simple" bacterium?

---

11. A. E. Wilder-Smith, *The Natural Sciences Know Nothing of Evolution*, T.W.F.T. Publishers, 1981, 82.
12. Mark Eastman and Chuck Missler, *The Creator Beyond Time and Space*, T.W.F.T. Publishers, 1996, 84.

No, let's just look at one part of a "simple" bacterium—its motility mechanism...

The so-called "bacterial flagellum" is what propels a bacterium through its microscopic world. The bacterial flagellum consists of about 40 different protein parts, including a stator, rotor, drive shaft, U-joint, and propeller. Through 21st century magnification technology, we now understand that a simple bacterium has a microscopic outboard motor! The individual parts come into focus when magnified 50,000 times using electron micrographs. These microscopic motors can run at 100,000 rpm. Nevertheless, they can stop on a microscopic dime. In fact, it takes only a quarter turn for them to stop, shift gears and start spinning 100,000 rpm in the other direction! The flagellar motor is water-cooled and hardwired into a sensory mechanism that allows the bacterium to get feedback from its environment![13]

This blows my mind! How does it compare with an outboard motor I'm familiar with? Was the mechanical motor designed and then manufactured according to engineered specifications? Of course! Now, make that same outboard motor one thousand times more efficient and miniaturize it by a factor containing many zeros. The complexity is staggering! Even with 21st century technology, we'll never be able to create a micro-machine like this.

Michael Behe, a biochemist currently teaching at Lehigh University, coined a term for describing the design phenomenon inherent in molecular machines such as the bacterial flagellar motor—"Irreducible Complexity"—*a single system composed of several well-matched, interacting parts that contribute to the basic function, wherein the removal of any one of the parts causes the system to effectively cease functioning.*[14]

Like a mechanical motor, each part in the flagellar motor is absolutely necessary for the whole to function. Therefore, I couldn't logically deduce any naturalistic, gradual, evolutionary explanation for the existence of a bacterial flagellum. Besides, no one would expect an outboard motor, whether mechanical or biological, to be the product of a chance assemblage of parts. Outboard motors are designed and engineered!

---

13. Various scientists, *Unlocking the Mystery of Life: The Scientific Case for Intelligent Design,*" DVD documentary by Illustra Media, 2002.
14. Michael J. Behe, *Darwin's Black Box: The Biochemical Challenge to Evolution,* Simon & Schuster, 1996, 39.

Of course, I just picked one example. The bacterial flagellum is only one among many thousands of intricate, well-designed, molecular machines. Furthermore, take these same principles of design and "irreducible complexity" and apply them to marvels such as the human eye, ear, heart, lungs and brain. Seriously, how can we logically explain the gradual and random development of these complex systems?

What about the human heart? It's a miraculously efficient and durable hydraulic pump that no engineer could dream of producing...

What about the human brain? It's a legitimate computer system, 1,000 times faster than a Cray supercomputer and with more connections than all the computers, phone systems and electronic appliances on the entire planet...[15]

Wait. I remember Darwin saying something about this...

> *If it could be demonstrated that any complex organ existed which could not possibly have been formed by numerous, successive, slight modifications, my theory would absolutely break down.*[16]

OK, using Darwin's own words, let's dig in further and look at one of these complex organs—the human eye...

The Complexity of the Eye & Other Organs

The human eye is enormously complicated—a perfect and interrelated system of about 40 individual subsystems, including the retina, pupil, iris, cornea, lens and optic nerve. For instance, the retina has approximately 137 million special cells that respond to light and send messages to the brain. About 130 million of these cells look like rods and handle the black and white vision. The other seven million are cone shaped and allow us to see in color. The retina cells receive light impressions, which are translated to electric pulses and sent to the brain via the

---

15. Eastman and Missler, *The Creator Beyond Time and Space*, 80.
16. Charles Darwin, *On the Origin of Species by Means of Natural Selection, or the Preservation of Favoured Races in the Struggle for Life* (referred to simply as "*Origin of Species*"), Bantam Books, 1999 (reprint of 1859 original), 158.

optic nerve. A special section of the brain called the visual cortex interprets the pulses to color, contrast, depth, etc., which allows us to see "pictures" of our world. Incredibly, the eye, optic nerve and visual cortex are totally separate and distinct subsystems. Yet, together, they capture, deliver and interpret up to 1.5 million pulse messages a milli-second! It would take dozens of Cray supercomputers programmed perfectly and operating together flawlessly to even get close to performing this task.[17]

That's so powerful to me! Obviously, if all the separate subsystems aren't present and performing perfectly at the same instant, the eye won't work and has no purpose. Logically, it would be impossible for random processes, operating through gradual mechanisms of natural selection and genetic mutation, to create 40 separate subsystems when they provide no advantage to the whole until the very last state of development and interrelation.

> *How did the lens, retina, optic nerve, and all the other parts in vertebrates that play a role in seeing suddenly come about? Because natural selection cannot choose separately between the visual nerve and the retina. The emergence of the lens has no meaning in the absence of a retina. The simultaneous development of all the structures for sight is unavoidable. Since parts that develop separately cannot be used, they will both be meaningless, and also perhaps disappear with time. At the same time, their development all together requires the coming together of unimaginably small probabilities.*[18]

The foregoing represents the core of "irreducible complexity." Complex organs made up of separate but necessary subsystems cannot be the result of random chance. Or, using the above language, such development could only result from "unimaginably small probabilities." For me, this means "statistical impossibility."

Come to think of it, I remember Darwin specifically discussing the incredible complexity of the eye in *Origin of Species*:

> *To suppose that the eye, with all its inimitable contrivances for adjusting the focus to different distances, for admitting different amounts of light, and for the correc-*

---

17.   Lawrence O. Richards, *It Couldn't Just Happen*, Thomas Nelson, Inc., 1989, 139-140.
18.   Dr. Ali Demirsoy, *Inheritance and Evolution*, Meteksan Publications, Ankara, 475.

tion of spherical and chromatic aberration, could have formed by natural selection, seems, I freely confess, absurd in the highest degree possible.[19]

So, how did Darwin deal with the staggering realities of the eye in the 1850's? As "absurdly" improbable as it was, he followed through with his theory and pointed to the simpler eye structures found in simpler creatures. He reasoned that more complex eyes gradually evolved from the simpler ones.

However, this hypothesis no longer passes muster. Short of the micro-biological and genetic information issues, paleontology now shows that "simple creatures" emerged in the world with complex structures already intact. Even the simple trilobite has an eye (complete with its double lens system) that's considered an optical miracle by today's standards.

Wait. The trilobite reminds me of something…Before I continue with the marvel of irreducible complexity and design, I have one more thought about Darwin and his original claims…

Transitional Forms and the Fossil Record

Let's start by looking at a few more of Darwin's very honest statements:

Firstly, why, if species have descended from other species by insensibly fine gradations, do we not everywhere see innumerable transitional forms? Why is not all nature in confusion instead of the species being, as we see them, well defined?[20]

But, as by this theory, innumerable transitional forms must have existed, why do we not find them embedded in countless numbers in the crust of the earth?[21]

Lastly, looking not to any one time, but to all time, if my theory be true, numberless intermediate varieties, linking closely together all the species of the same group, must assuredly have existed.[22]

Why then is not every geological formation and every stratum full of such intermediate links? Geology assuredly does not reveal any such finely graduated organic

---

19.   Darwin, *Origin of Species*, 155.
20.   Ibid., 143.
21.   Ibid., 144.
22.   Ibid., 149.

chain; and this, perhaps is the most obvious and gravest objection which can be urged against my theory.[23]

Since Darwin put forth his original theory, scientists have sought fossil evidence indicating past organic transitions. Nearly 150 years later, there has been no evidence of evolutionary transition found thus far in the fossil record. In Darwin's own words, if his theory of "macro-evolution" were true, we would see a vast number of fossils at intermediate stages of biological development. In fact, based on standard mathematical models, we would see far more transitional forms in the fossil record than complete specimens. However, we see none—not one true transitional specimen has ever been found.

Our museums now contain hundreds of millions of fossil specimens (40 million alone are contained in the Smithsonian Natural History Museum). If Darwin's theory were true, we should see at least tens of millions of unquestionable transitional forms. We see none. Even the late Stephen Jay Gould, Professor of Geology and Paleontology at Harvard University and the leading spokesman for evolutionary theory prior to his recent death, confessed "the extreme rarity of transitional forms in the fossil record persists as the trade secret of paleontology."[24]

He continues:

> *The history of most fossil species includes two features inconsistent with gradualism: 1. Statis. Most species exhibit no directional change during their tenure on earth. They appear in the fossil record looking much the same as when they disappear...2. Sudden Appearance. In any local area, a species does not arise gradually by the steady transformation of its ancestors; it appears all at once and 'fully formed'.*[25]

> *The evolutionary trees that adorn our textbooks have data only at the tips and nodes of their branches; the rest is inference, however reasonable, not the evidence of fossils.*[26]

Wait. I need to tighten this down! Are there *some* transitional fossils, or *none*? If Gould uses phrases like "extreme rarity" and "most species exhibit no directional change" when referring to the fossil record, that must mean that there are at least some transitional specimens. Right?

---

23. Ibid., 230.
24. *Natural History* 86(5), 1977, 14.
25. Ibid., 13.
26. Gould, "Evolution's Erratic Pace", *Natural History*, Vol. 5, 1977.

Author Luther Sunderland saw the same issue, so he determined to get the definitive answer from the top museums themselves. Sunderland interviewed five respected museum officials, recognized authorities in their individual fields of study, including representatives from the American Museum, the Field Museum of Natural History in Chicago, and the British Museum of Natural History. None of the five officials were able to offer a single example of a transitional series of fossilized organisms that document the transformation of one Kind of plant or animal into another.[27]

The British Museum of Natural History boasts the largest collection of fossils in the world. Among the five respected museum officials, Sunderland interviewed Dr. Colin Patterson, Senior Paleontologist at the British Museum and editor of a prestigious scientific journal. Patterson is a well known expert having an intimate knowledge of the fossil record. He was unable to give a single example of Macro-Evolutionary transition. In fact, Patterson wrote a book for the British Museum of Natural History entitled, "Evolution". When asked why he had not included a single photograph of a transitional fossil in his book, Patterson responded:

> *...I fully agree with your comments on the lack of direct illustration of evolutionary transitions in my book. If I knew of any, fossil or living, I would certainly have included them. You suggest that an artist should be used to visualize such transformations, but where would he get the information from? I could not, honestly, provide it, and if I were to leave it to artistic license, would that not mislead the reader? I wrote the text of my book four years ago. If I were to write it now, I think the book would be rather different. Gradualism is a concept I believe in, not just because of Darwin's authority, but because my understanding of genetics seems to demand it. Yet Gould and the American Museum people are hard to contradict when they say there are no transitional fossils. As a paleontologist myself, I am much occupied with the philosophical problems of identifying ancestral forms in the fossil record. You say that I should at least "show a photo of the fossil from which each type of organism was derived." I will lay it on the line—there is not one such fossil for which one could make a watertight argument.[28]*

OK, I just wanted to complete that loop. In my research, I haven't found even one transitional fossil. Therefore, based on Darwin's own words, his original theory of macro-evolutionary progression didn't happen. Paleontology was a brand

---

27. Colin Patterson, personal communication. Luther Sunderland, *Darwin's Enigma: Fossils and Other Problems*, 4th edition, 1988, 88-90.
28. Ibid.

new scientific discipline in the mid-1800's, and now, roughly 150 years later, we know that the fossil record doesn't provide the support Darwin himself required.

David B. Kitts. PhD (Zoology) is Head Curator of the Department of Geology at the Stoval Museum. In an evolutionary trade journal, he wrote:

> *Despite the bright promise that paleontology provides a means of "seeing" evolution, it has presented some nasty difficulties for evolutionists, the most notorious of which is the presence of "gaps" in the fossil record. Evolution requires intermediate forms between species and paleontology does not provide them...*[29]

N. Heribert Nilsson, a famous botanist, evolutionist and professor at Lund University in Sweden, continues:

> *My attempts to demonstrate evolution by an experiment carried on for more than 40 years have completely failed...The fossil material is now so complete that it has been possible to construct new classes, and the lack of transitional series cannot be explained as being due to scarcity of material. The deficiencies are real, they will never be filled.*[30]

Even the popular press is catching on. This is from an article in *Newsweek* magazine:

> *The missing link between man and apes, whose absence has comforted religious fundamentalists since the days of Darwin, is merely the most glamorous of a whole hierarchy of phantom creatures...The more scientists have searched for the transitional forms that lie between species, the more they have been frustrated.*[31]

And one last thought:

> *In the years after Darwin, his advocates hoped to find predictable progressions...these have not been found—yet the optimism has died hard, and some pure fantasy has crept into textbooks.*[32]

So, what would Darwin say today?

---

29. *Evolution*, vol. 28, 467.
30. Nilsson quoted in *The Earth Before Man*, p. 51.
31. "Is Man a Subtle Accident," *Newsweek*, November 3, 1980.

*Now, after over 120 years of the most extensive and painstaking geological explora-
tion of every continent and ocean bottom, the picture is infinitely more vivid and
complete than it was in 1859. Formations have been discovered containing hundreds of billions of fossils and our museums are filled with over 100 million fossils
of 250,000 different species.*

*The availability of this profusion of hard scientific data should permit objective
investigators to determine if Darwin was on the right track. What is the picture
which the fossils have given us?...The gaps between major groups of organisms*

---

32. David M. Raup, "Evolution and the Fossil Record," *Science*, vol. 213, July 1981,
     289.

The reality of the human fossil record of the past century:

Ramapithecus was widely recognized as a direct ancestor of humans. It is now established that he was merely an extinct type of orangutan.
Piltdown man was hyped as the missing link in publications for over 40 years. He
was a fraud based on a human skull cap and an orangutan's jaw.
Nebraska man was a fraud based on a single tooth of a rare type of pig.
Java man was based on sketchy evidence of a femur, skull cap and three teeth found
within a wide area over a one year period. It turns out the bones were found in an
area of human remains, and now the femur is considered human and the skull cap
from a large ape.
Neandertal man was traditionally depicted as a stooped ape-man. It is now accepted
that the alleged posture was due to disease and that Neandertal is just a variation of
the human kind.
Australopithecus afarensis, or "**Lucy**," has been considered a missing link for years.
However, studies of the inner ear, skulls and bones have shown that she was merely
a pygmy chimpanzee that walked a bit more upright than some other apes. She was
not on her way to becoming human.
Homo erectus has been found throughout the world. He is smaller than the average
human of today, with a proportionately smaller head and brain cavity. However, the
brain size is within the range of people today and studies of the middle ear have
shown that he was just like current Homo sapiens. Remains are found throughout
the world in the same proximity to remains of ordinary humans, suggesting coexist-
ence. **Australopithecus africanus** and **Peking man** were presented as ape-men missing links for years, but are now both considered Homo erectus.
Homo habilis is now generally considered to be comprised of pieces of various other
types of creatures, such as Australopithecus and Homo erectus, and is not generally
viewed as a valid classification.

have been growing even wider and more undeniable. They can no longer be ignored or rationalized away with appeals to imperfection of the fossil record.[33]

Thanks for indulging that little side bar. Now, back to our 21st century understanding of micro-biology, genetics and design theory…

Design Theory

OK, where am I with all this?

Evolutionary theory declares that everything has a mere appearance of design. Richard Dawkins, author of *The Blind Watchmaker* and a professor at Oxford University (U.K.), is probably the leading proponent of evolutionary theory since the death of Stephen Jay Gould.

Dawkins writes:

> *Biology is the study of complicated things that give the appearance of having been designed for a purpose.*[34]

He goes on to say:

> *…the living results of natural selection overwhelmingly impress us with the appearance of design as if by a master watchmaker…*[35]

Nevertheless, Dawkins is an atheist who staunchly maintains that the design we see is merely an illusion—that these amazingly complex systems are an accidental product of natural selection.

Interestingly, in all other fields of human endeavor we find that "design necessitates a designer." Thus, design detection methodology is a prerequisite for many disciplines, including archaeology, anthropology, forensics, criminal jurisprudence, copyright law, patent law, reverse engineering, crypto-analysis, random number generation, and SETI (the Search for Extra-Terrestrial Intelligence). In general, we find "specified complexity" to be a reliable indicator of the presence

---

33. Luther D. Sutherland, *Darwin's Enigma: Fossils and Other Problems*, 4th edition, Master Books, 1988, 9.
34. Richard Dawkins, *The Blind Watchmaker*, ch. 1.
35. Richard Dawkins, *The Blind Watchmaker*, ch. 2.

of intelligent design. Chance can explain complexity, but not specification. A random sequence of letters is complex, but not specified (it is meaningless). A Shakespearean sonnet is both complex and specified (it is meaningful). You can't have a Shakespearean sonnet without Shakespeare.[36]

Remarkably, the SETI project, a multi-billion dollar effort to scan the cosmos for some indication of intelligence, is based on one simple notion. If we find radio waves that contain any type of ordered sequence of sounds, then we've discovered intelligence somewhere in the universe! Think about that? The whole premise of these scientists is that you can't have ordered sound (such as the blips and dashes in a Morse code transmission) without an intelligent force behind them. To me, that's huge!

Charles B. Thaxton, PhD in Chemistry and Postdoctoral Fellow at Harvard University, agrees:

> *...an intelligible communication via radio signal from some distant galaxy would be widely hailed as evidence of an intelligent source. Why then doesn't the message sequence on the DNA molecule also constitute prima facie evidence for an intelligent source? After all, DNA information is not just analogous to a message sequence such as Morse code, it is such a message sequence.*[37]

So, where is this going? It appears to me, if we shed our prior preconceptions and logically examine our organic world—like we do most everything else—we start to see things differently...

Intelligent Design & Machines

So, how do I connect the dots between the organic and inorganic world? Intelligent Design is obvious upon close examination of any mechanical machine. The concept and design inherent in a machine, whether simple or complex, is self-evident. Whether a machine is high quality or low quality, its designer is both necessary and apparent. Information Theory states that concept and design can only result from a mind. Even the diminished quality of a poorly constructed machine cannot obscure the necessity of an intelligent designer.

---

36. William A. Dembski, *The Design Inference: Eliminating Chance through Small Probabilities*, 1998.
37. Charles B. Thaxton, *The Mystery of Life's Origin: Reassessing Current Theories*, Philosophical Library, 1984.

Machines, as defined by French Biochemist and Nobel Laureate Jacques Lucien Monod (1910–1976), are "purposeful aggregates of matter that, utilizing energy, perform specific tasks."[38] By this authoritative definition, living systems are also recognized as machines. A living organism fulfills the definition of a machine all the way down to the molecular level.

Back in the mid-1700's, David Hume successfully invalidated the "machine" analogy in biologic systems because we could only guess at what existed at the molecular level.[39] However, the phenomenal discoveries in the last few decades have finally and unequivocally demonstrated that living systems are, in fact, machines—even to the deepest, molecular level![40]

> *It has only been over the past twenty years with the molecular biological revolution and with the advances in cybernetic and computer technology that Hume's criticism has been finally invalidated and the analogy between organisms and machines has at last become convincing...In every direction the biochemist gazes, as he journeys through the weird molecular labyrinth, he sees devices and appliances reminiscent of our own twentieth-century world of advanced technology.[41]*

Because of the metaphysical implications of life resulting from Intelligent Design, a surprisingly large number of us seek to reject the foregoing statements and find a mechanism by which complex biologic machines may arise naturally by random chance.

However, I was now seeing a tremendous inconsistency...

> *When it comes to the origin of life there are only two possibilities: creation or spontaneous generation. There is no third way. Spontaneous generation was disproved one hundred years ago, but that leads us to only one other conclusion, that of supernatural creation. We cannot accept that on philosophical grounds; therefore, we choose to believe the impossible: that life arose spontaneously by chance![42]*

---

38.   For Monod's theories see A. E. Wilder-Smith, *The Natural Sciences Know Nothing of Evolution*, T.W.F.T. Publishers, 1981; and Eastman and Missler, *The Creator Beyond Time and Space*, 43.

39.   David Hume, *Dialogues Concerning Natural Religion*, Fontana Library Ed., Collins, 1779.

40.   Eastman and Missler, *The Creator Beyond Time and Space*, 79.

41.   Denton, *Evolution: A Theory in Crisis*, 340.

42.   George Wald, "The Origin of Life," *Scientific American*, 191:48, May 1954.

Sir Arthur Keith, a famous British evolutionary anthropologist and anatomist, declares:

> *Evolution is unproved and unprovable. We believe it only because the only alternative is special creation, and that is unthinkable.*[43]

H.S. Lipson, a Professor of Physics at the University of Manchester (UK), continues:

> *In fact, evolution became in a sense a scientific religion; almost all scientists have accepted it, and many are prepared to 'bend' their observations to fit with it.*[44]

Statistics and Impossibility

So, I'm going to look at this one more time...

Could life evolve randomly from inorganic matter? Not according to mathematicians.

> *In the last 30 years a number of prominent scientists have attempted to calculate the odds that a free-living, single-celled organism, such as a bacterium, might result by the chance combining of pre-existent building blocks. Harold Morowitz calculated the odds as one chance in $10^{100,000,000,000}$. Sir Fred Hoyle calculated the odds of only the proteins of an amoebae arising by chance as one chance in $10^{40,000}$.*
>
> *...the odds calculated by Morowitz and Hoyle are staggering. The odds led Fred Hoyle to state that the probability of spontaneous generation 'is about the same as the probability that a tornado sweeping through a junk yard could assemble a Boeing 747 from the contents therein.' Mathematicians tell us that any event with an improbability greater than one chance in 10^{50} is in the realm of metaphysics—i.e. a miracle.*[45]

Harold Marowitz, an atheist physicist, created mathematical models by imagining broths of living bacteria that were superheated until all the complex chemicals were broken down into basic building blocks. After cooling the mixtures, Marowitz used physics calculations to conclude that the odds of a single bacte-

---

43. David Hume, *Dialogues Concerning Natural Religion* (1779).
44. H.S. Lipson, "A Physicist Looks at Evolution," *Physics Bulletin*, vol. 31, May 1980, 138.
45. Mark Eastman, MD, *Creation by Design*, T.W.F.T. Publishers, 1996, 21-22.

rium reassembling by chance is one in $10^{100,000,000,000}$.[46] Wow! How can I grasp such a large statistic? Well, it's more likely that I would win the state lottery every week for a million years by purchasing just one ticket each week.

In response to the probabilities calculated by Marowitz, Robert Shapiro, author of *Origins—A Skeptic's Guide to the Creation of Life on Earth*, wrote:

> *The improbability involved in generating even one bacterium is so large that it reduces all considerations of time and space to nothingness. Given such odds, the time until the black holes evaporate and the space to the ends of the universe would make no difference at all. If we were to wait, we would truly be waiting for a miracle.*[47]

Sir Fred Hoyle compared the probability of life arising by chance to lining up 10^{50} (ten with fifty zeros after it) blind people, giving each one a scrambled Rubik's Cube, and finding that they all solve the cube at the same moment.[48]

Regarding the origin of life, Francis Crick, winner of the Nobel Prize in biology for his work with the DNA molecule, stated in 1982:

> *An honest man, armed with all the knowledge available to us now, could only state that in some sense, the origin of life appears at the moment to be almost a miracle, so many are the conditions which would have had to have been satisfied to get it going.*[49]

A Final "Experiment"

Remarkably, right before I finished this chapter, a friend confronted me with "proof" that life had been created in a "random" laboratory experiment. After a little discussion, I realized that my buddy was pointing to the "spark and soup" experiments of the 1950's where guys like Harold Urey and Stanley Miller passed mixtures of boiling water, ammonia, methane and hydrogen through elaborate "electric spark systems" of beakers and test tubes. In those experiments, they were able to produce traces of one or two amino acids—the "building blocks of

---

46. Eastman and Missler, *The Creator Beyond Time and Space*, 76-77.
47. Robert Shapiro, *Origins—A Skeptic's Guide to the Creation of Life on Earth*, 1986, 128.
48. Fred Hoyle, *The Intelligent Universe*, Holt, Rinehart and Winston, 1983, 11.
49. Francis Crick, *Life Itself—Its Origin and Nature*, Futura, 1982.

life"—and therefore, the media hailed these as proof for the possibility of spontaneous generation on a prebiotic Earth.[50]

There were many unreported problems with these "designed" experiments. Dramatically, the greatest byproducts of these soups were tar (85%) and carboxylic acids (13%), both of which are toxic to living systems. Notwithstanding all the other issues, producing a trace amino acid in a laboratory experiment would be similar to producing a clay brick and declaring that we just figured out how to randomly design and build a New York skyscraper.

After discussing a little more of the science stuff, I turned to my friend and decided to toss him a nice graphic illustration…

"Take a frog and put him in a blender. Turn the blender on for seven minutes, or until whipped to a frothy consistency."

He stared at me with that look…

"Pour the mixture into an open container and place the container in the sun for a few million years. After a few million years, retrieve the container and examine the contents…"

I gave him a nod, "Do you have a frog?"

He thought for only a second…

"Nope, you still have frog soup," he laughed.

"You're absolutely right," I agreed. "How can you have anything but a soupy mixture containing the building blocks of frog life. With no information code to tie it all together, you have nothing resembling any kind of self-existing organism."

In this simple (yet graphic) illustration, I gave every potential to create a frog. I provided every chemical, amino acid, protein and molecule that makes up the frog's organic structure. However, if I placed this illustration in the context of a "prebiotic soup" on primitive Earth, we'd be lucky to see even one trace element

---

50. See, Harold C. Urey, *The Planets, Their Origin and Development*, Yale University Press, 1952; and Stanley Miller, *Science*, vol. 117, 1953, 528-529.

or amino acid develop over the same time period—let alone the biologic components of an entire frog!

Exploring My World from an Impartial View

If *matter acting on matter for a sufficient period of time can create anything*, then I should be able to go out to the Mountains of Colorado and find naturally-occurring computers, cameras, and cell phones. As we've seen, those inorganic devices are much less complex than a "simple" organic bacterium. Yet, most people would find my statement to be "silly" at best. Why? Whether organic or inorganic, the complexity and design is obvious.

To take this concept to a simple level, I examined the watch on my wrist (mine is digital). I contemplated the interdependent system of silicon chips, wires, and LED displays? Actually, by today's technological standards, that's a pretty simple device. However, is there any question that it was created by a group of designers, handed off to a team of mechanical engineers, and then placed into production by a team of automation specialists?

Then I took a minute to look at the wrist under my watch. I've grown comfortable with its apparent simplicity. I looked closer at the skin and hair follicles. I touched them. I thought about the nerves that just told my brain to synthesize that touch. Then I focused more closely and pondered the microscopic makeup of each of my cells. I imagined the complex cellular city at work, and contemplated the wonder of my brain that allowed me to imagine such a thing. I thought about the veins just under the surface of my skin. I thought about my heart pumping oxygenated blood through those veins to keep my wrist and hand alive. I thought about my lungs as they inflated, deflated, and processed that oxygen for my heart.

Then I flexed my hand. I pondered the miraculous communication effort that occurred in a milli-second. I created a thought—my brain processed the subconscious instruction and translated it into a task for my body—my nervous system delivered that task to my wrist—and my wrist performed the task perfectly. I never really thought about what just happened? How does an interconnected system like that evolve gradually and randomly over time?

It goes on and on…My digestive tract—How did that evolve gradually over millions of years? Without processed energy, how would my earliest, evolving ancestors even exist? My part in a two-part reproductive system—Come on, how did that evolve randomly over millions of years through natural selection and genetic mutation? How do you pass on new and improved genetic traits without the means to reproduce in the first place? I was finally thinking about these things!

So, out of all this, I developed a new thesis for my view of life...We need to drop our preconceived notions. Dump our presuppositions. Just meditate on this material with an impartial mind. Does this stuff have "metaphysical" implications? Sure. But why should that deter us from logically examining the evidence? Where did we get the notion that science and technology somehow have to exist in a naturalistic vacuum? That's not true science. True science is observing the evidence, creating a hypothesis, and testing that hypothesis through various means. Philosophical presuppositions have no place in true science. If science reveals things outside the bounds of known physics, then science should be applauded for its impartial contribution to philosophical and metaphysical thought.

I. L. Cohen is a mathematician, researcher and author—a member of the New York Academy of Sciences and officer of the Archaeological Institute of America. In his book, *Darwin was Wrong—A Study in Probabilities*, Cohen writes:

> *In a certain sense, the debate transcends the confrontation between evolutionists and creationists. We now have a debate within the scientific community itself; it is a confrontation between scientific objectivity and ingrained prejudice—between logic and emotion—between fact and fiction.*[51]

> *...In the final analysis, objective scientific logic has to prevail—no matter what the final result is—no matter how many time-honored idols have to be discarded in the process.*[52]

> *...after all, it is not the duty of science to defend the theory of evolution, and stick by it to the bitter end—no matter what illogical and unsupported conclusions it offers...if in the process of impartial scientific logic, they find that creation by outside superintelligence is the solution to our quandary, then let's cut the umbilical cord that tied us down to Darwin for such a long time. It is choking us and holding us back.*[53]

---

51. I. L. Cohen, *Darwin was Wrong—A Study in Probabilities*, New Research Publications, Inc., 1984, 6-7.
52. Ibid., 8.
53. Ibid., 214-215.

...every single concept advanced by the theory of evolution (and amended thereafter) is imaginary and it is not supported by the scientifically established facts of microbiology, fossils, and mathematical probability concepts. Darwin was wrong.[54]

...The theory of evolution may be the worst mistake made in science.[55]

54. Ibid., 209.
55. Ibid., 210.

Now What?

For me, logic screamed that someone (or something) was responsible for life. Now, I couldn't go back. To be intellectually honest with myself, I had to go forward and discover who (or what) caused everything that I see. It could be God…it could be Mother Nature…it could be UFO's—but it was something…

To be honest, I was very uncomfortable—I didn't like the "metaphysical" implications of what science and technology revealed. For me, evolution was dead. The world did not create itself. Therefore, my comfortable humanist, materialist worldview also had to die. Since someone (or something) was out there, logic declared that my relativistic view of things also had to go…

Although skeptical about my next subject, I had to keep searching…I started reading the various myths, stories and histories about our past. I studied the ancient civilizations. I reviewed maps of the ancient world. I was fascinated by the archaeological evidence. In fact, I had no idea mankind was writing government records, statutory codes and legal contracts in 2500 BC. I thought ancient history was merely oral traditions of very simple cultures. Then, I started reading the so-called "holy books"…

FURTHER STUDY SUGGESTIONS—PART I

Charles Darwin, *On the **Origin of Species** by Means of Natural Selection, or the Preservation of Favoured Races in the Struggle for Life* (referred to simply as "*Origin of Species*"), Bantam Books, 1999 (reprint of 1859 original).

The publication of Darwin's "Origin of Species" in 1859 marked a dramatic turning point in scientific thought. Actually, this book revolutionized science, philosophy and theology by asserting the theory of natural selection. Contrary to centuries of scientists before him, Darwin reasoned that species were not created all at once by a divine hand, but started with a few simple forms that mutated and adapted over time. "Origin of Species" is probably the most influential book ever written in the natural sciences.

Michael J. Behe, ***Darwin's Black Box**: The Biochemical Challenge to Evolution*, Simon & Schuster, 1996.

The foundation for evolutionary changes must occur at the molecular level before they can change an organism, and by extension a species. If this is not occurring, as Behe persuasively argues, then natural selection is incapable of guiding the process, and a designer must be posited to explain the development of life on the molecular level. Behe is not a creationist, and stops short of calling the designer God, but he provides a very compelling argument for the necessity of intelligent design. Behe looks at the so-called machines that are responsible for processes like vision or blood-clotting, and examines whether they can be explained by random mutation or natural selection. His answer, from years of molecular study, is that the design involved in each process is too great and "irreducibly complex."

Various scientists, ***Unlocking the Mystery of Life**: The Scientific Case for Intelligent Design*, DVD, Illustra Media, 2002.

Did life on Earth—with all its incredible complexity and diversity—arise from an undirected evolutionary process, as many scientists have believed since the time of Darwin? Or was something else at work? Until recently, Darwin's theory has gone relatively unchallenged by the scientific community. But now, powerful new evidence points to an exciting explanation known as the theory of intelligent design. This is a fascinating journey into the interior of living cells, DNA, and molecular machines that point to overwhelming evidence of intelligent design. Featuring state-of-the-art computer animation and insights from leading scientists.

Michael Denton, ***Evolution: A Theory in Crisis***, Adler and Adler Publishers, Inc., 1985.

A molecular biologist shows how rapidly accumulating evidence is threatening the basic assumptions of orthodox Darwinism. Although the theory appears to be correct regarding micro-evolutionary changes, its larger claims to account for the relationship between classes and orders, let alone the origin of life, appear to be based on shaky foundations at best. Not only has paleontology failed to come up with the fossils which Darwin anticipated, but hypothetical reconstructions of major evolutionary developments—such as linking birds to reptiles—are beginning to look more like fantasies than serious conjectures.

Jonathan Wells, ***Icons of Evolution***: *Science or Myth?* Faithworks Publications, 2001.

Berkeley-educated doctor of biology, Jonathan Wells, lets you in on scientific discoveries you won't learn about from high school and college textbooks. The best-known "icons" of evolution—from pictures of apes evolving into humans, to comparisons of fish and human embryos, to moths on tree trunks—are fraudulent or misleading. For decades, biology students have been taught things about evolution that are simply untrue. These icons of evolution appear even in the most recent textbooks, although the scientific literature is full of evidence that they are false.

William A. Dembski, ***Intelligent Design***: *The Bridge Between Science & Theology*, InterVarsity Press, 1999.

A pivotal work from one of the leading theorists in the Intelligent Design movement! Arguing that intelligent design is a crucial link between science and theology, Dembski addresses controversial issues such as the discernment of divine action in nature, the significance of miracles, intellectual challenges to naturalistic evolutionary theories, intelligent design as a theory of information, and more.

Phillip E. Johnson, ***Darwin on Trial***, InterVarsity Press, 1993.

Is Darwin's theory of evolution really established scientific fact? Johnson, a Berkeley law professor specializing in logic, dissects Darwinism's scientific support and finds it woefully short on logic and severely lacking in confirmatory evidence. This rigorous—yet readable—book is a great introduction to the controversy over evolution vs. creation.

PART II

THE INTEGRITY OF THE BIBLE

Reading the Bible as an "Intellectual Exercise"

For me, the Bible was no different than the other ancient religious books—a mere translation of an interpretation of an interpolation of an oral tradition—and therefore, a book with no credibility or connection to the ancient manuscripts (if they even existed at all). Before this journey began, I had no interest in reading this "convoluted" mythology book. However, I was really enjoying my study of archaeology, and the archaeology books kept referring to the Bible as an historical and geographical resource. Therefore, I felt the need to at least read the Bible as an "intellectual exercise" to help connect the dots with respect to people, places and events mentioned in the other books I was reading...

Well, I was stunned!

No, really!

So many of us think we've read the Bible, but when it comes down to it, we really haven't. Of course, I remembered a few of the stories, and even memorized a couple of verses, but I hadn't actually read the perennial best seller cover to cover like a Michener novel. Well, I highly recommend it—if for no other reason than to read the most-widely published and distributed book of all time.

The Bible as a History Book

The Bible is a phenomenal account of history, comprised of 66 separate books, written over approximately 1,600 years, by at least 40 distinct authors. The Old Testament contains 39 books written from approximately 1500 to 400 BC, and the New Testament contains 27 books written from approximately 40 to 90 AD. The Jewish Bible (*Tanakh*) is the same as the Christian Old Testament, except for its book arrangement. The original Old Testament was written mainly in Hebrew, with some Aramaic, while the original New Testament was written in common Greek.

The Bible begins with the Jewish Scriptures. The historical record of the Jews was written down on leather scrolls and tablets over centuries, and the authors included kings, shepherds, prophets and other leaders. The first five books are called the Law, which were written and/or edited primarily by Moses in the early 1400's BC. Thereafter, other scriptural texts were written and collected by the Jewish people during the next 1,000 years. About 450 BC, the Law and the other Jewish Scriptures were arranged by councils of rabbis (Jewish teachers), who then recognized the complete set as the inspired and sacred authority of God (Elohim). At some time during this period, the books of the Hebrew Bible were arranged by topic, including the Law (*Torah*), the Prophets (*Nebiim*), and the Writings (*Ketubim*). The first letters of these Hebrew words—T, N and K—form the name of the Hebrew Bible—the *Tanakh*.[1]

Beginning as early as 250 BC, the Hebrew Bible was translated into Greek by Jewish scholars in Alexandria, Egypt. This translation became known as the "Septuagint," meaning 70, and referring to the tradition that 70 (probably 72) men comprised the translation team. It was during this process that the order of the books was changed to the order we have in today's Bible: Historical (Genesis—Deuteronomy), poetic (Job—Song of Songs), and prophetic (Isaiah—Malachi).[2]

Although the Jewish Scriptures were copied by hand, they were extremely accurate copy to copy. The Jews had a phenomenal system of scribes, who developed intricate and ritualistic methods for counting letters, words and paragraphs to insure that no copying errors were made. These scribes dedicated their entire lives to preserving the accuracy of the holy books. A single copy error would require the immediate destruction of the entire scroll. In fact, Jewish scribal tradition was maintained until the invention of the printing press in the mid-1400's AD. As far as manuscript accuracy, the recent discovery of the Dead Sea Scrolls has confirmed the remarkable reliability of this scribal system over thousands of years[3] (I'll get back to the Dead Sea Scrolls later).

---

1. Henry H. Halley, *Halley's Bible Handbook*, 25th ed., Zondervan Publishing House, 2000, 1071.
2. Ibid.
3. Various, *Zondervan Handbook to the Bible*, Zondervan Publishing House, 1999, 64-65.

After approximately 400 years of scriptural silence, Jesus arrived on the scene in about 4 BC. Throughout his teaching, Jesus often quotes the Old Testament, declaring that he did not come to destroy the Jewish Scriptures, but to fulfill them. In the Book of Luke, Jesus proclaims to his disciples, "all things must be fulfilled which were written in the Law of Moses and the Prophets and the Psalms concerning Me."[4]

Starting in about 40 AD, and continuing to about 90 AD, the eye-witnesses to the life of Jesus, including Matthew, Mark, Luke, John, Paul, James, Peter and Jude, wrote the Gospels, letters and books that became the Bible's New Testament. These authors quote from 31 books of the Old Testament, and widely circulate their material so that by about 150 AD, early Christians were referring to the entire set of writings as the "New Covenant." During the 200s AD, the original writings were translated from Greek into Latin, Coptic (Egypt) and Syriac (Syria), and widely disseminated as "inspired scripture" throughout the Roman Empire (and beyond).[5] In 397 AD, in an effort to protect the scriptures from various heresies and offshoot religious movements, the current 27 books of the New Testament were formally and finally confirmed and "canonized" in the Synod of Carthage.[6]

The Manuscript Evidence

I was genuinely surprised! I really thought the Bible was a great read! It had exciting stories, war strategy, foreign intrigue…What else could anyone want from an ancient "religious book"…?

But, come on, what about its credibility as a history book? I mean, what about all of the changes made to the Bible over the centuries? What about all those interpretations and interpolations of the oral tradition? At best, how can I read the Bible as anything but a fun novel?

The first thing I discovered was a common misunderstanding about interpretations and translations. Yes, the Bible has been translated from its original lan-

---

4.   Luke 24:44, *The Holy Bible, New King James Version*, Thomas Nelson Publishers, 1982.
5.   F.F. Bruce, *The New Testament Documents: Are They Reliable?* 5th rev. ed., Intervarsity Press, 1960, 21-28.
6.   Ibid., 27.

guages, but it has not been changed, interpreted or interpolated along the way. Translations such as the King James Version are derived from existing copies of ancient manuscripts—the Hebrew *Masoretic Text* (Old Testament) and the Greek *Textus Receptus* (New Testament). Today's Bibles are not translations of texts translated from other interpretations—they go right back to the ancient source manuscripts. The primary differences between today's Bible translations are merely related to how translators interpret a word or sentence from the original language (Hebrew, Aramaic and Greek). This is no different than any other book we read in English that was translated from a different source language.

Dramatically, when the Bible is compared to other writings, it stands alone as the best-preserved literary work of all antiquity. Remarkably, there are thousands of existing Old Testament manuscripts and fragments copied throughout the Middle East, Mediterranean and European regions that agree phenomenally with each other.[7] In addition, these texts substantially agree with the Septuagint version of the Old Testament, which was translated from Hebrew to Greek some time during the 3rd century BC.[8] The Dead Sea Scrolls, discovered in Israel in the 1940's and 50's, also provide astounding evidence for the reliability of the ancient transmission of the Jewish Scriptures (Old Testament) in the 1st, 2nd and 3rd centuries BC.[9]

The manuscript evidence for the New Testament is also dramatic, with nearly 25,000 ancient manuscripts discovered and archived so far, at least 5,600 of which are copies and fragments in the original Greek.[10] Some manuscript texts date to the early second and third centuries, with the time between the original autographs and our earliest existing fragment being a remarkably short 40-60 years.[11]

Interestingly, this manuscript evidence far surpasses the manuscript reliability of other ancient writings that we trust as authentic every day. Look at these comparisons: Julius Caesar's *The Gallic Wars* (10 manuscripts remain, with the earliest

---

7.   Josh McDowell, *The New Evidence that Demands a Verdict*, Thomas Nelson Publishers, 1999, 71-73.

8.   Josh McDowell, *Evidence that Demands a Verdict*, vol.1, Thomas Nelson Publishers, 1979, 58-59.

9.   Ibid. 56-57.

10.   McDowell, *The New Evidence that Demands a Verdict*, 34-36.

11.   *John Ryland's Gospel of John fragment*, John Ryland's Library of Manchester, England. See also, Ibid., 38.

one dating to 1,000 years after the original autograph); Pliny the Younger's *Natural History* (7 manuscripts; 750 years elapsed); Thucydides' *History* (8 manuscripts; 1,300 years elapsed); Herodotus' *History* (8 manuscripts; 1,350 years elapsed); Plato (7 manuscripts; 1,300 years); and Tacitus' *Annals* (20 manuscripts; 1,000 years).[12]

Renowned Bible scholar F.F. Bruce declares:

> *There is no body of ancient literature in the world which enjoys such a wealth of good textual attestation as the New Testament.*[13]

Homer's *Iliad*, the most renowned book of ancient Greece, is the second best-preserved literary work of all antiquity, with 643 copies of manuscript support discovered to date. In those copies, there are 764 disputed lines of text, as compared to 40 lines in all the New Testament manuscripts.[14] In fact, many people are unaware that there are no surviving manuscripts of any of William Shakespeare's 37 plays (written in the 1600's), and scholars have been forced to fill some gaps in his works.[15] This pales in textual comparison with the over 5,600 copies and fragments of the New Testament in the original Greek that, together, assure us that nothing's been lost. In fact, all of the New Testament except eleven minor verses can be reconstructed outside the Bible from the writings of the early church leaders in the second and third centuries AD.[16]

> *In real terms, the New Testament is easily the best attested ancient writing in terms of the sheer number of documents, the time span between the events and the document, and the variety of documents available to sustain or contradict it. There is nothing in ancient manuscript evidence to match such textual availability and integrity.*[17]

The academic discipline of "textual criticism" assures us that the Bible translations we have today are essentially the same as the ancient manuscripts, with the

---

12. McDowell, *Evidence that Demands a Verdict*, vol.1, 42.

13. F.F. Bruce, *The Books and the Parchments: How We Got Our English Bible*, Fleming H. Revell Co., 1950, 178.

14. Norman L. Geisler and William E. Nix, *A General Introduction to the Bible*, Moody, Chicago, Revised and Expanded 1986, 366-67.

15. http://shakespeare.com/faq/, Dana Spradley, Publisher, 2002.

16. McDowell, *Evidence that Demands a Verdict*, vol. 1, 50-51.

17. Ravi K. Zacharias, *Can Man Live Without God?* Word Publishing, 1994, 162.

exception of a few inconsequential discrepancies that have been introduced over time through copyist error. We must remember that the Bible was hand-copied for hundreds of years before the invention of the first printing press. Nevertheless, the text is exceedingly well preserved. Again, I pondered this—of the approximately 20,000 lines that make up the entire New Testament, only 40 lines are in question. These 40 lines represent one quarter of one percent of the entire text and do not in any way affect the teaching and doctrine of the New Testament. I again compared this with Homer's *Iliad*. Of the approximately 15,600 lines that make up Homer's classic, 764 lines are in question. These 764 lines represent over 5% of the entire text, and yet nobody seems to question the general integrity of that ancient work.

To my real surprise, I discovered the Bible to be better preserved—by far—than other ancient works I've read and accepted over the years, such as Homer, Plato and Aristotle. As far as my "interpretation of an interpolation of an oral tradition" theory, I found that the Bible was not changed or interpreted from the ancient source texts. Simply, as the Bible was carried from country to country, it was translated into languages that don't necessarily mirror the original languages of Greek, Hebrew and Aramaic. However, other than some grammatical and cultural differences, the Bible is absolutely true to its original form and content, and remarkably well-preserved in its various translations.

The Archaeological Evidence

I must say, I really enjoyed reading the Bible as a history book. Now that I was secure in its translation integrity, I dug in and absorbed its presentation of the ancient world. The Bible appeared much different than the other "holy books" I was perusing, which seemed to focus on philosophy and notions of transcendentalism. The writers of the Bible seemed to have a solid grasp on the people, places and events of history.

Smack. I had another "Wait a Minute" moment...

What about the scholars that discredit the historical veracity of the Bible based on a lack of archaeological evidence for various civilizations, cities, and leaders mentioned in the Old Testament. In my archaeology studies, these "academics" seemed to pop up from time to time—and I have to say, they sounded pretty credible. I decided to retreat a bit from the Bible, and went back to my archaeology books...

Ancient Mesopotamian Cultures

One of the most revealing things about studying archaeology is realizing that the scientific discipline really didn't exist until about 150 years ago. Archeology wasn't even a "soft" science prior to the 19th century—it was merely treasure hunting conducted by self-seeking opportunists. Therefore, many excavations were botched and many discoveries were lost. With the rise in academic interest and the proliferation of technological tools, a systematic approach to archaeology has taken off in the last century, revealing a great deal about the ancient world.

So, what have they discovered about Old Testament times…?

Since I was always trying to reconcile ancient maps with today's maps, I decided to start by looking at the archaeological evidence for the cities and civilizations mentioned in the Bible. How about the early cities of Abraham and the Patriarchs? Did they really exist? Abraham's ancestral home of "Ur" is presented as a powerful city-state in southern Mesopotamia—it's mentioned four times in the Old Testament. Well, it turns out Ur is located in modern Iraq. Depending on strife in the region, it has been excavated on and off during the last century, exposing a wealth of information about the pagan culture of Abraham's time. In the Book of Genesis, Abraham's father, Terah, moved his family north to "Haran."[18] This ancient city has been discovered and excavated in modern-day Turkey. Also found in that same area of Turkey are villages that still have the names of Abraham's grandfather and great grandfather, Nahor and Serug.[19]

To date, numerous sites and artifacts have been uncovered that reveal a great deal about the ancient Mesopotamian culture. One of the most dramatic finds is the "Sumerian King List," which dates to approximately 2100 BC. This collection of clay tablets and prisms is most exciting because it divides the Sumerian kings into two categories; those who reigned before the "great flood" and those who reigned after it.[20] Actually, records of a global flood are found throughout most ancient cultures. For instance, the "Epic of Gilgamesh" from the ancient Babylonians contains an extensive flood story. Discovered on clay tablets in locations such as

---

18. Genesis 11:31. See Alfred Hoerth, *Archaeology and the Old Testament*, Baker Books, 1998, 59-72.
19. Genesis 11:22.
20. Hoerth, *Archaeology and the Old Testament*, 188.

Ninevah and Megiddo, the Epic even includes a man who built a great ship, filled it with animals, and used birds to see if the water had receded.[21]

Archaeology in the last century has also shed light on the great military civilizations of ancient Mesopotamia and their ultimate impact on law and culture throughout the region. One significant find is the "Law Code of Hammurabi," which is a seven foot tall, black diorite carving containing about 300 laws of Babylon's King Hammurabi. Dated to about 1750 BC, the Law Code contains many civil laws that are similar to those found in the first five books of the Bible. Another dig at the ancient city of "Nuzi" near the Tigris River uncovered approximately 20,000 clay tablets. Dated between 1500 and 1400 BC, these cuneiform texts explain the culture, customs and laws of the time, many of which are similar to those found in the early books of the Bible.[22]

As far as major ancient empires, the Hittite civilization is mentioned throughout the Old Testament as ruling the area of present-day Turkey, Syria and Lebanon, yet nothing was known of these people outside of the Bible. About 100 years ago, ancient "Boghazkoy" was discovered east of Ankara, Turkey, which revealed itself as the expansive capital city of the Hittite Empire. Since then, archaeologists have uncovered a wealth of information about the history, language and culture of a people considered "imaginary" by many scholars until the 1900's.[23]

The Bible tells us a great deal about Nebuchadnezzar and the Babylonian Empire, which destroyed Jerusalem in 586 BC and exiled the Jews to Babylon for 70 years. Well, ancient Babylon has now been uncovered, comprising nearly 3,000 acres about 55 miles south of current-day Baghdad in Iraq. The ruins include the famous ziggurat structures, the Palace of King Nebuchadnezzar, and the enormous walls that measured 80 feet thick (wide enough to allow a four-horse chariot to make a full turn on the top of the wall).[24]

The Philistines were known as one of the "Sea Peoples" that constantly warred against the Israelites for control of early Canaan. Mentioned over 200 times in

---

21.   Ibid., 192-96. See also, Genesis, chapters 7 & 8.
22.   Randall Price, *The Stones Cry Out: What Archaeology Reveals About the Truth of the Bible*, Harvest House Publishers, 1997, 92-94. See also, Hoerth, *Archaeology and the Old Testament*, 119, 102.
23.   Pat Zukeran, *Archaeology and the Old Testament*, Probe Ministries, www.probe.org/docs/arch-ot.html, 2003, 2-3. See also, Price, *The Stones Cry Out*, 82-83.
24.   Hoerth, *Archaeology and the Old Testament*, 372-378.

the Old Testament, the Philistines had a major fortified seaport at Ashkelon on the Mediterranean Sea, which was discovered just north of present-day Gaza. Nebuchadnezzar destroyed Ashkelon in 604 BC, as predicted by Jeremiah and other Old Testament prophets.[25]

I was really impressed! Call me totally naïve, but I had no idea that all these places mentioned in the Bible truly existed! I dug in more...

Ancient Israel

Since I was looking at the ancient cities and cultures mentioned in the Bible, I guess the ones with ultimate significance would be those related to ancient Israel. So that's where I focused next. Mentioned more than 50 times in the Bible, Jericho was the initial entry point into the "Promised Land" for the Israelite people.[26] Archaeology has now confirmed the location of this fortified city of walls and towers that guarded entry to the land of Canaan from the east.[27] Shechem was also an important city throughout the Old Testament. In fact, King Jeroboam made it the capital of the northern kingdom of Israel in the 10th century BC.[28] Excavations have uncovered huge walls and a fortified gate system containing such important finds as the temple of Baal from the biblical story of Abimelech.[29]

Excavations in the north have also revealed the city of Dan, which was a Canaanite stronghold conquered by Israel (specifically, the tribe of Dan) around 1150 BC.[30] The rebuilt city, which became the northern boundary of Israel, has delivered a wealth of artifacts with biblical importance.[31] The southern boundary of Israel was Beersheba, which became a fortified city during the period of King Solomon.[32] Excavations between 1969 and 1976 have revealed massive walls, gates, wells and storehouses consistent with biblical accounts.[33] The ancient city

---

25. Ibid., 233-234.
26. Joshua 6.
27. Zukeran, *Archaeology and the Old Testament*, 4-5. Hoerth, *Archaeology and the Old Testament*, 209-210. Price, *The Stones Cry Out*, 52-53.
28. 1 Kings 12:25.
29. Judges 9:46.
30. Judges 18.
31. Price, *The Stones Cry Out*, 227-230.
32. 1 Kings 4:25.
33. Hoerth, *Archaeology and the Old Testament*, 285.

of Jerusalem, dating to the time of King David's initial conquest, was discovered and excavated between 1978 and 1985. Prior to this time, nothing apart from the Bible was known about King David's Jerusalem, which has now revealed a palace, towers and the famous Siloam spring.[34] The ancient ruins of Gibeah were discovered about three miles north of Jerusalem. Gibeah was the home to Saul and the tribe of Benjamin, and later became King Saul's capital city.[35] Excavations have revealed Saul's fortress palace dated to about 1100 BC.[36]

Megiddo was a Canaanite city conquered by Israel in the north. It was a walled fortress that sat on a hill near an expansive plain that witnessed many battles of historical significance. In the 900s BC, King Solomon fortified the city,[37] and later in the 600s BC, King Josiah lost a battle to the Egyptians there.[38] Megiddo (also known as Armageddon) has now been extensively excavated, revealing such treasures as the Canaanite religious "high places" mentioned throughout the Old Testament.[39]

I was never disappointed! I found that the archaeological evidence for the ancient cities mentioned in the Bible was absolutely compelling. OK, but what about the evidence for the ancient Israelites themselves? Some scholars propose that the ancient Canaanites existed in these cities, but the Israelites didn't come on the scene until centuries after the Bible declares.

I continued my exploration...

The "Merneptah Stele" (also known as the Israel Stele) is an upright stone slab measuring over seven feet tall that contains carved hieroglyphic text dating to approximately 1230 BC. This Egyptian monument describes the military victories of Pharaoh Merneptah and includes the earliest mention of "Israel" outside the Bible. Although the specific battles covered by the stele are not included in the Bible, the stele establishes outside evidence that the Israelites were already living as a people in ancient Canaan by 1230 BC.[40] In addition to the Stele, a large

---

34. Price, *The Stones Cry Out*, 164-165. See, 2 Samuel and 1 Chronicles.
35. Judges 19 and 1 Samuel 10-15.
36. Hoerth, *Archaeology and the Old Testament*, 248-250.
37. 1 Kings 4.
38. 2 Kings 23.
39. Hoerth, *Archaeology and the Old Testament*, 87, 205-06.
40. Price, *The Stones Cry Out*, 145-146. Hoerth, *Archaeology and the Old Testament*, 228-229.

wall picture was discovered in the great Karnak Temple of Luxor (ancient Thebes), which shows battle scenes between the Egyptians and Israelites. These scenes have also been attributed to Pharaoh Merneptah and date to approximately 1209 BC.[41] The Karnak Temple also contains records of Pharaoh Shishak's military victories about 280 years later. Specifically, the "Shishak Relief" depicts Egypt's victory over King Rehoboam in about 925 BC, when Solomon's Temple in Judah was plundered.[42] This is the exact event mentioned in two books of the Old Testament.[43]

Outside Egypt, we also discover a wealth of evidence for the early Israelites. The "Moabite Stone" (Mesha Stele) is a three-foot stone slab discovered near Dibon, east of the Dead Sea that describes the reign of Mesha, King of Moab, around 850 BC.[44] According to the Book of Genesis, the Moabites were neighbors of the Israelites.[45] This stele covers victories by King Omri and King Ahab of Israel against Moab, and Mesha's later victories on behalf of Moab against King Ahab's descendants.[46] The "Black Obelisk of Shalmaneser" is a seven-foot, four-sided pillar of basalt that describes the victories of King Shalmaneser III of Assyria, including defeats of Tyre, Sidon and "Jehu, Son of Omri." Dated to about 841 BC, the Obelisk (now in the British Museum) was discovered in the Northwest Palace at Nimrud and shows Israel's King Jehu kneeling before the Assyrian king in humble tribute.[47]

OK, everything I found establishes that the ancient Israelites did in fact exist. However, there's a big difference between historic generalities and the specific people and events mentioned in the Bible. For instance, King David and his son, Solomon, are huge parts of Jewish history in the Old Testament. Shouldn't we find archeological support for their reigns and activities as well?

In one of the books I picked up, I was surprised to read that the historical David never existed. Another article I read referred to the well-established "David Myth"—a literary invention drawn from heroic tradition to establish the Jewish monarchy...

---

41. Hoerth, *Archaeology and the Old Testament*, 230.
42. Ibid., 301-302.
43. 1 Kings 14 and 2 Chronicles 12.
44. Hoerth, *Archaeology and the Old Testament*, 308-310.
45. Genesis 19.
46. 2 Kings 3.
47. Hoerth, *Archaeology and the Old Testament*, 321-22. See also, 2 Kings 9-10.

Kathleen Kenyon, a very credible archaeologist I came to trust and enjoy, declared:

> *To many people it seems remarkable that David and Solomon still remain unknown outside the Old Testament or literary sources derived directly from it. No extra-biblical inscription, either from Palestine or from a neighboring country, has yet been found to contain a reference to them.*[48]

Well, I guess we don't have to find archaeological evidence for every person and place mentioned in the Bible, but David was huge to me. I discovered he's mentioned 1,048 times in the Bible—the subject of 62 chapters and the writer of probably 73 Psalms in the Old Testament. Boy, I really wanted to see some evidence for that guy...

Guess what? Since Kenyon made the above statement in roughly 1987, the validity of the ancient biblical record regarding King David received a huge lift!

In 1993, archaeologists discovered a stone inscription at the ancient city of Dan, which refers to the "House of David." The "House of David Inscription" (Tel Dan Inscription) is the first ancient reference to King David outside the Bible.[49] Specifically, the stone is a victory pillar of a King in Damascus dated a couple hundred years after David's reign, which mentions a "king of Israel of the House of David." Over the next year, more inscription pieces were discovered at the site, which allowed archaeologists to reconstruct the entirety of the declaration: "I killed Jehoram son of Ahab king of Israel and I killed Ahaziahu son of Jehoram king of the House of David." Remarkably, these are Jewish leaders linked to the lineage of David as recorded in the Bible.[50]

It just goes on and on...Event after event...Reference after reference...The biblical record of history never disappointed me...

The defeats of Samaria and Ashdod to Sargon II, king of Assyria, as recorded on his palace walls.[51] The military campaign of the Assyrian king Sennacherib

---

48.   Kathleen Kenyon, *The Bible and Recent Archaeology*, rev. ed., John Knox Press, 1987, 85.
49.   Price, *The Stones Cry Out*, 166-67.
50.   Ibid. 167-72.
51.   Hoerth, *Archaeology and the Old Testament*, 342-343. See 2 Kings 17:3-6, 24; 18:9-11; and Isaiah 20:1.

against Judah, as recorded on the Taylor Prism.[52] The siege of Lachish by Sennacherib, as recorded on the Lachish Reliefs.[53] The destruction of Nineveh as predicted by the prophets Nahum and Zephaniah, as recorded on the Tablet of Nabopolasar.[54] The defeat of Jerusalem by Nebuchadnezzar, king of Babylon, as recorded in the Babylonian Chronicles.[55] The Babylonian captivity of Jehoiachin, king of Judah, as recorded in the Babylonian Ration Records.[56] The defeat of Babylon by the Medes and Persians, as recorded on the Cyrus Cylinder.[57] The freeing of the Jewish captives from Babylon by Cyrus the Great, as recorded on the Cyrus Cylinder.[58]

The palace at Jericho where Eglon, king of Moab, was assassinated by Ehud. The east gate of Shechem where Gaal and Zebul watched the forces of Abimelech approach the city. The Temple of Baal in Shechem, where the citizens of Shechem took refuge when Abimelech attacked the city. The pool of Gibeon where the forces of David and Ishbosheth fought during the struggle for the kingship of Israel. The royal palace at Samaria where the kings of Israel lived. The Pool of Samaria where King Ahab's chariot was washed after his death. The water tunnel beneath Jerusalem dug by King Hezekiah to provide water during the Assyrian siege. The royal palace in Babylon where King Belshazzar held the feast and Daniel interpreted the handwriting on the wall. The royal palace, gate and square at Susa where the events of Esther, the queen to the Persian king Xerxes, and Mordecai, her cousin, took place.[59]

Wow! Only a century and a half ago, European academics in the "Age of Enlightenment" declared that the Bible (especially the Old Testament) was fictional his-

---

52. Price, *The Stones Cry Out*, 272. See 2 Kings 18:13-16.
53. Ibid., 79-81. Hoerth, *Archaeology and the Old Testament*, 351. See 2 Kings 18:14, 17.
54. Bryant Wood, *Associates for Biblical Research*, 2001, http://www. christiananswers.net/q-abr/abr-a009.html. See Nahum 3:7 and Zephaniah 2:13-15.
55. Price, *The Stones Cry Out*, 232-233. See 2 Kings 24:10-14.
56. Wood, *Associates for Biblical Research*, http://www.christiananswers.net/q-abr/abr-a009.html. See 2 Kings 24:15-16.
57. Price, *The Stones Cry Out*, 250-252. See Daniel 5:30-31.
58. Ibid. See Ezra 1:1-4; 6:3-4.
59. Bryant Wood, *Associates for Biblical Research*, 1995-2001, http:// christiananswers.net/q-abr/abr-a005.html; http://christiananswers. net/q-abr/jericho.html. Scripture citations, in order, Judges 3:15-30; Judges 9:34-38; Judges 9:4, 46-49; 2 Samuel 2:12-32; 1 Kings 20:43; 21:1, 2; 22:39; 2 Kings 1:2; 15:25; 1 Kings 22:29-38; 2 Kings 20:20; 2 Chronicles 32:30; Daniel 5; and the Book of Esther.

tory. Their primary rationale was that empires such as the Hittites, and kings such as David, didn't really exist. Well, now we have dramatic archaeological support for their existence! Moreover, in recent years, the archaeological finds have increased dramatically! Therefore, if the rationale for rejecting Old Testament scripture was lack of corroborating historical and archaeological evidence, shouldn't the same rationale exist for validating the Old Testament record now that we're finding such evidence?

Although the general strife in the Middle East has slowed archaeological endeavors somewhat, the Bible's reliability as an historical document continues to be confirmed by the field of archaeology every day. Although absence of archaeological evidence does not necessarily mean absence of the people, place or event, it may be stated emphatically that no archaeological discovery has ever refuted a Biblical reference.

Dr. Nelson Glueck, probably the greatest modern authority on Israeli archeology, has said:

> *No archeological discovery has ever controverted a single biblical reference. Scores of archeological findings have been made which confirm in clear outline or exact detail historical statements in the Bible. And, by the same token, proper evaluation of Biblical descriptions has often led to amazing discoveries.*[60]

For me, this was really becoming an unexpected and exciting journey...

New Testament Support

OK, that research helped me dramatically with the historical veracity of the Old Testament, but what about the New Testament? The Old Testament was maintained as the historical archives for an entire nation by a well-organized system of recorders and scribes. However, wasn't the New Testament merely a collection of religious books and letters written by a few independent zealots trying to encourage followers after the death of their religious leader?

At this point, I was on fire for exploring this stuff. Nobody ever told me this material was available. I thought the Bible was a collection of moral mythology stories used to support "blind faith" in a couple of major world religions. I had no

---

60.   Nelson Glueck, *Rivers in the Desert*, Farrar, Strous and Cudahy, 1959, 136.

idea that the Bible was grounded in historical, geographical and archaeological evidence. As I turned to the evidence for the New Testament writings, I was reading and digesting up to four books per week...

Guess what? It was remarkable! Like the Old Testament, I found that the historical record of the New Testament was upheld again and again...

The foundations of the Jewish Temple Mount built by Herod the Great still stand in Jerusalem. The "Southern Steps" where Jesus and his followers entered the Temple are preserved in an active excavation site. The Church of the Nativity in Bethlehem is generally considered a credible site for the birth place of Jesus. The huge Church of the Holy Sepulcher in Jerusalem is also considered a reliable historical site covering the locations of the crucifixion and burial of Christ. These sites were covered over (and thus, preserved) by the Romans in the second century AD.

On the Sea of Galilee, towns such as Nazareth are still active. Capernaum and Chorazin, two sites Jesus visited often, have been excavated and preserved. Sites of famous teachings such as Kursi (the swine miracle), Tabgha (loaves and fishes), Mount of Beatitudes (Sermon on the Mount) and Caesarea Philippi (Peter's confession) are all preserved as reliable historical sites.

I was spending hours at my desk with the latest archaeology books and periodicals, cross-referencing the latest finds with the New Testament passages...It was fascinating...

The synagogue at Capernaum where Jesus cured a man with an unclean spirit and delivered the sermon on the bread of life. The house of Peter at Capernaum where Jesus healed Peter's mother-in-law and others. Jacob's well where Jesus spoke to the Samaritan woman. The Pool of Bethesda in Jerusalem, where Jesus healed a crippled man. The Pool of Siloam in Jerusalem, where Jesus healed a blind man. The tribunal at Corinth where Paul was tried. The theater at Ephesus where the riot of silversmiths occurred. Herod's palace at Caesarea where Paul was kept under guard.[61] It went on and on...

---

61. Bryant Wood, *Associates for Biblical Research*, 1995-2001, http:// christiananswers.net/q-abr/abr-a005.html#nt See also, Price, *The Stones Cry Out*, 295-318. Scripture citations, in order, Mark 1:21-28 and John 6:25-59; Matthew 8:14-16; John 4; John 5:1-14; John 9:1-4; Acts 18:12-17; Acts 19:29; and Acts 23:33-35.

Of course, none of this archaeological evidence proved the underlying theology to me, but it was still powerful. The places existed and the historical events happened. I wasn't convinced of the miraculous extent of these events, but there was nothing denying their historicity…

I was ready to go one layer deeper and see who these history writers were. In my mind, I needed to further establish their credibility in order to start understanding where they were coming from with their record of such profound events…

The Writer Named Luke

I decided to start with Luke, because that's where the archaeologists and historians seemed to start. Also, Luke wrote about one-quarter of the New Testament (his Gospel account and the Book of Acts), so, for me, that was a big enough chunk of text to start testing the veracity of the entire New Testament.

Starting about 150 years ago, scholars in Europe started rejecting the historical records of Luke. These academics declared that there was no evidence to support the existence of several locations and leaders mentioned in Luke's writings, and therefore, they rejected the entirety of his account. However, I discovered that archaeological finds during the last century have revealed that Luke was a very accurate historian and the two books he authored were absolutely authoritative records of history!

One of the greatest archaeologists of all time was Sir William Ramsay. He studied under the famous German historical schools in the mid-nineteenth century, which taught that the New Testament was a religious treatise written in the mid-200s AD, and not an historical document recorded in the first century. Ramsay was so convinced of this teaching that he entered the field of archaeology and went to Asia Minor to specifically find the physical evidence to refute Luke's biblical record. After years of field study, Ramsay completely reversed his entire view of the Bible and first century history. He wrote:

> *Luke is a historian of the first rank; not merely are his statements of fact trustworthy, he is possessed of the true historic sense…in short, this author should be placed along with the greatest of historians.*[62]

---

62. Sir William M. Ramsey, *The Bearing of Recent Discovery on the Trustworthiness of the New Testament*, Hodder & Stoughton, 1915.

Luke's accuracy is demonstrated by the fact that he names key historical figures in the correct time sequence. He also uses the correct, and often obscure, government titles in various geographical areas, including the politarchs of Thessalonica, the temple wardens of Ephesus, the procouncil of Cyprus, and the "first man of the island" in Malta. In Luke's announcement of Jesus' public ministry, he mentions, "Lysanius tetrarch of Abilene". Scholars questioned Luke's credibility since the only Lysanius known for centuries was a leader of Chalcis who ruled from 40–36 BC. However, an inscription dated to the time of Tiberius (14–37 AD) was found, which records a temple dedication naming Lysanius as the "tetrarch of Abila" (Abilene near Damascus). This matched Luke's account and stunned the liberal scholarship of the day.[63]

In the Book of Acts, Paul was brought before Gallio, the proconsul of Achaea. Again, archaeology confirms this account. At Delphi, an inscription from Emperor Claudius was discovered that says, "Lucius Junios Gallio, my friend, and the proconsul of Achaia..." Historians date the inscription to 52 AD, which supports the time of Paul's visit there in 51 AD.[64]

Later in Acts, Erastus, a coworker of Paul, is appointed treasurer of Corinth. In 1928, archaeologists excavated a Corinthian theatre and discovered an inscription that reads, "Erastus in return for his aedilship laid the pavement at his own expense." The pavement was laid in 50 AD, and the term "aedile" refers to the designation of treasurer.[65]

In another passage, Luke gives Plubius, the chief man on the island of Malta, the title, "first man of the island." Scholars questioned this strange title and deemed it unhistorical. Inscriptions have recently been discovered on the island that indeed give Plubius the title of "first man."[66]

Elsewhere, Luke uses the Greek term "politarchs" ("rulers of the city") to refer to the leaders in Thessalonica. Although it sounds inconsequential, this was another hit against Luke's credibility for centuries, because no other Greek literature used this leadership term. However, approximately 20 inscriptions have now been dis-

63. Pat Zukeran, Archaeology and the New Testament, 2000, 4, http://www.probe.org/docs/arch-nt.html. Scripture citation: Luke 3:1.
64. Ibid. Scripture citation: Acts 18:12-17.
65. Ibid. Scripture citation: Acts 19:22.
66. Ibid. Scripture citation: Acts 28:7.

covered that bear the term "politarch," including five finds that specifically refer to the ancient leadership in Thessalonica.[67]

As a final example, Luke calls Iconium a city in Phyrigia. Who cares? Well, this was also a major rub against the credibility of Luke for centuries. Scholars, going all the way back to writings from historians like Cicero, maintained that Iconium was in Lycaonia, not Phyrigia. Therefore, scholars declared that the entire Book of Acts was unreliable. Guess what? In 1910, Ramsay was looking for the evidence to support this long-held claim against Luke and he uncovered a stone monument declaring that Iconium was indeed a city in Phyrigia.[68] Many archaeological discoveries since 1910 have confirmed this—Luke was right!

Famous historian A.N. Sherwin-White declares:

> *In all, Luke names thirty-two countries, fifty-four cities, and nine islands without error.*[69]

> *For Acts the confirmation of historicity is overwhelming.... Any attempt to reject its basic historicity must now appear absurd.*[70]

I'll end with this one—Luke's opening to the Christmas story that many of us are familiar with...

> *And it came to pass in those days that a decree went out from Caesar Augustus that all the world should be registered. This census first took place while Quirinius was governing Syria. So all went to be registered, everyone to his own city.*[71]

In this passage, we learn of a decree from Caesar Augustus that all the world will be taxed and everyone must return to their home city for a formal census. We also read that this concept of registration and taxation was first decreed when Quirinius (also known as Cyrenius) was governing Syria. Well, for centuries, this whole text was considered a fabrication, since there was no secular record of such

---

67. Eric Lyons, *Luke and the Term Politarchas*, Apologetic Press, 2002, http://www.apologeticspress.org/rr/rr2002/res0204b.htm. Scripture citation: Acts 17:6.

68. "The Book of Acts," *New Testament Introductions*. The Blue Letter Bible. 2002-04. http://www.blueletterbible.org/study/intros/acts.html. Scripture citation: Acts 14:6.

69. Norman Geisler, *Baker Encyclopedia of Apologetics*, Baker Books, 1999, 47.

70. A. N. Sherwin-White, *Roman Society and Roman Law in the New Testament*, Clarendon Press, 1963, 189.

71. Luke 2:1-3, *The Holy Bible, New King James Version*.

a Roman census or that people had to return to their home cities. Also, the only record of Quirinius (Cyrenius) being "governor" of Syria was 6–7 AD (Josephus), much too late to coincide with the biblical record.

Guess what? Recent discoveries reveal that the Romans did have a regular enrollment of taxpayers and held a formal census every 14 years, beginning with the reign of Caesar Augustus.[72] In addition, an inscription and other archaeological evidence reveal that Quirinius was indeed "governing" Syria around 7 BC (although not with the official title of "governor", he was the military leader in the territory).[73] Finally, a papyrus discovered in Egypt generally discusses the system of Roman taxation, declaring the following: "Because of the approaching census it is necessary that all those residing for any cause away from their home should at once prepare to return to their own governments in order that they may complete the family registration of the enrollment..."[74]

I had to admit, Luke passed my notion of a "credibility test." In fact, his style was far from the religious fanaticism that I expected. Like me, his whole point for writing his accounts was to collect the evidence and present the historical "case" for Jesus and his teachings. For me, it was powerful that Luke writes his entire text as a research paper—"an orderly account"—for a Roman official named Theophilus. Here's the beginning of Luke's record:

> *Having carefully investigated all of these accounts from the beginning, I have decided to write a careful summary for you, to reassure you of the truth of all you were taught.*[75]

So, as an authoritative writer of history, Luke passed my test with flying colors. I wasn't ready to accept his theology, but I wasn't really "testing" that yet. I was still checking out the authenticity and credibility of these guys...

---

72. E. M. Blaiklock, "Quirinius," *The Zondervan Pictorial Encyclopedia of the Bible*, vol. 5, Zondervan Publishing House, 1976, 6. See also, http://users.rcn.com/tlclcms/census.html#Anchor4.

73. Ronald Marchant, *The Census of Quirinius: The Historicity of Luke 2:1-5*, Interdisciplinary Biblical Research Institute, Research Report #4, 1980, 4-6, http://www.ibri.org/04census.htm.

74. See: http://users.rcn.com/tlclcms/census.html#Anchor4. Cited in Maier, Fullness, 4, who is quoting from A. H. M. Jones, ed., *A History of Rome through the Fifth Century*, Harper and Row, 1970, II, 256f.

75. Luke 1:3-4, New Living Translation, Tyndale House Publishers, 1996.

Who was next on the list...?

The Writer Named John

John also wrote a big chunk of the New Testament, including his Gospel, letters, and the Book of Revelation, so that's where I went next...Again, I wasn't focusing on the "theological stuff" yet—I just wanted to test the "historical" elements first...

Well, I soon discovered that John's accuracy is also supported by recent discoveries.

In the Gospel of John, Jesus heals a man at the Pool of Bethesda. John describes the pool as having five porticoes.[76] Until recently, this site was a point of scholarly skepticism. Then, 40 feet underground, archaeologists discovered a pool with five porticoes, and a surrounding area that perfectly matches John's description.[77] Later in the text, John describes the Pool of Siloam,[78] another site of contention for hundreds of years. Well, archaeologists discovered this pool in 1897.[79]

Further in John's Gospel, John describes Pontius Pilate speaking to Jesus from the judgment seat in a place called "the Pavement" ("Gabbatha" in Hebrew).[80] For hundreds of years, scholars used this "myth" to reject John's record of Jesus and the trial by Pilate, because there was no historical record of a court called Gabbatha or "the Pavement" in Jerusalem. However, famous archaeologist William Albright revealed that this place was in fact the court of the Tower of Antonia, which was destroyed by the Romans in 66–70 AD. It was left buried when Jerusalem was rebuilt in the time of Hadrian, but it was recently uncovered during excavations there.[81]

OK, that's great stuff for "site support," but what about some of these "larger-than-life" characters such as Pontius Pilate, the procurator of Rome who presided over the trial of Jesus?

---

76.   John 5:1-15.
77.   http://www.digbible.org/tour/bethesda.html.
78.   John 9:7.
79.   http://www.bible-history.com/jerusalem/
       firstcenturyjerusalem_pool_of_siloam.html.
80.   John 19:13.
81.   William Albright, *The Archaeology of Palestine*, Penguin Books, 1960.

Well, in 1961, archaeologists discovered a plaque fragment in Caesarea, a Roman city along the Mediterranean coast of Israel. The plaque was written in Latin and imbedded in a section of steps leading to Caesarea's Amphitheatre. The inscription includes the following: "Pontius Pilatus, Prefect of Judea has dedicated to the people of Caesarea a temple in honor of Tiberius." Emperor Tiberius reigned from 14 to 37 AD, perfectly meshing with the New Testament account that records Pontius Pilate ruling as governor from 26 to 36 AD.[82]

Tacitus, a well-known first century Roman historian, also mentioned Pontius Pilate:

> *Christus, from whom the name had its origin, suffered the extreme penalty during the reign of Tiberius at the hands of one of our procurators, Pontius Pilatus...*[83]

Wait. Did I read this right? A Roman historian not only mentions a Roman governor, Pontius Pilate, but he also mentions Christus—Christ—and his suffering at the hands of Pilate! For me, this was huge! I was always taught that Jesus Christ and the events of the New Testament were solely contained in the Bible.

I was blown away...! Are there other ancient writings outside the Bible mentioning New Testament people and events—even Jesus Himself?

I made a big star in my notes...I was definitely coming back to this one...!

OK, now what...?

All of this stuff happened—historically, I mean...I still didn't accept the theological implications of these events, but they obviously happened nonetheless...They weren't myths...They weren't hoaxes...They were historical events.

So, how could I start testing the depths of these events? What drove the writers of the Bible to such passion? What compelled these men to write and defend such profound messages in connection with these historical events?

Come on! Were there really divine underpinnings to all of these books? Intellectually, I now knew something "metaphysical" was out there...More than "meta-

---

82. Price, *The Stones Cry Out*, 307-308.
83. Tacitus, *Annales, Historiae*, Chapter 15, paragraphs 54.

physical"—something with intelligence. But, could I really accept that these books were from outside our dimensions of time and space...?

I was ready to accept the Bible as a very special book. I was even ready to declare its historical trustworthiness. But the notion of "divine inspiration" still seemed a little over the edge to me. I just couldn't get my skeptical mind around that one...

If God truly delivered this book from outside our four dimensions, wouldn't he just tell us? I understand that the writers of the Bible say it's divinely inspired, but that's not enough for me. It just seems that if God truly delivered this book to mankind through a group of 40 or so authors that he would give us something to hang our hats on...Yes, I'm stunned by the Bible's historical veracity, archaeological support, internal integrity, etc.—the evidence is fantastic, and definitely sets the Bible apart—but how could I ever be asked to jump the chasm from "really special book" to "divinely inspired letter from God"?

The Test of Prophecy

Well, I discovered that the Bible took care of this! I found that the Bible itself declares the test for divine inspiration! The test is established as 100% fulfilled prophecy.[84]

In all candor, when I read this, I kind of laughed...Yeah right...this is the test of the tabloid press too...Whenever a major world event happens, people love the hype of prophecy and urban legend. The tabloids love to showcase the ancient (and not-so-ancient) prophecies of Nostradamus, Jean Dixon, Edgar Cayce and the Bible...Why was the Bible lumped together with all that goofiness...? These so-called prophets get one thing right, and the public could care less about all their other predictive failures. What a game...

Wait. The Bible declares that its test for supernatural inspiration is <u>100%</u> fulfilled prophecy. That means no predictive failures whatsoever. Wow, that's really remarkable. <u>100%</u>. No misses. I really had to absorb that. Would the multi-billion dollar gambling and lottery industries exist today if people could legitimately and consistently tell the future? Of course not. Maybe this prophecy thing wasn't as laughable as I first thought.

---

84.   Deuteronomy 18:20:22. See also, Deuteronomy 13:1-5 and 2 Peter 1:20-21.

OK, I guess the power in the Bible's 100% fulfillment standard is directly proportional to the number of prophecies declared in the Bible. Obviously, 100% of two isn't that staggering...I decided to carefully and honestly study the prophetic scriptures...

Historic Prophecy

With the help of some study aides, I discovered over 1,000 prophecies in the Bible. Of those, an astonishing 668 of them have been fulfilled and none have ever proven false (three seem to be unconfirmed). The others focus on events that are supposed to take place in the future. Come on! These must be generalized, self-fulfilling predictions that find their fulfillment within the pages of the same book. One religious zealot writes a prediction (God will do something specific and dramatic) and another writes the fulfillment (God did something specific and dramatic). The predictions and fulfillments are confined to the pages of the same "holy book." Not too meaningful...Where's the outside support? What does secular history say, if anything, about these events?

I decided to take a hard, calculated look at some of the Bible's historical prophecies...

The Decree of Cyrus

In about 700 BC, Isaiah names Cyrus as the king who will allow the Israelites to return to Jerusalem and rebuild its Temple.[85] At the time of this prophecy, there was no king named Cyrus and the Temple in Jerusalem was totally built and in full operation.

In 586 BC, more than 100 years later, the Babylonian King Nebuchadnezzar sacked Jerusalem and destroyed the temple. The Jews living in Jerusalem were either killed or taken captive to Babylon.[86] In about 539 BC, the Babylonian Empire was conquered by the Persians. Shortly thereafter, a Persian king named Cyrus issued a formal decree that the Jews could return to Jerusalem and rebuild their temple.[87] This decree is confirmed by secular archaeology in the form of a

---

85. Isaiah 44:28; 54:1.
86. McDowell, *Evidence that Demands a Verdict*, vol. 2, 346.
87. 2 Chronicles 36:22-23.

stone cylinder that details many events of Cyrus' reign, including the decree to rebuild the Temple in Jerusalem.[88]

Remarkably, Isaiah predicted that a man named Cyrus, who would not be born for about a hundred years, would give a decree to rebuild a city and a temple, which were still standing and fully active at the time!

I had to check more of these out...!

The City of Tyre

In 586 BC (confirmed by secular sources as the 11th year of the reign of King Zedekiah of Judah), Ezekiel predicts the fall of mainland Tyre to the Babylonian armies of Nebuchadnezzar.[89] The text further describes the siege against the island fortress of Tyre (a half mile off the coast of mainland Tyre) hundreds of years later. Ezekiel's prophecy describes how the future invaders would tear down the ruins of mainland Tyre and throw them into the sea. They would "scrape her dust from her and leave her as the top of a rock".[90] "They will lay your stones, your timber, and your soil in the midst of the water." "I will make you like the top of a rock; you shall be a place for spreading nets."[91]

Secular history records that Nebuchadnezzar laid siege to the great mainland city of Tyre about a year after Ezekiel's prophecy. The *Encyclopedia Britannica* says: "After a 13-year siege (585–573 BC) by Nebuchadnezzar II, Tyre made terms and acknowledged Babylonian suzerainty."[92] When Nebuchadnezzar broke through the city gates, he found it nearly empty. Most of the people had moved by ship to an island about a half mile off the coast and fortified a city there. The mainland city was destroyed in 573 BC (Ezekiel's first prediction), but the city of Tyre on the island remained a powerful city for several hundred years.

Secular history next records that Alexander the Great laid siege to the island fortress of Tyre in 332 BC. His army destroyed the remains of mainland Tyre and threw them into the Mediterranean Sea. As Alexander's army constructed a causeway to the island, they scraped even the dust from the mainland city, leav-

---

88.   McDowell, *Evidence that Demands a Verdict*, vol. 2, 347.
89.   Ezekiel 26.
90.   Ezekiel 26:4.
91.   Ezekiel 26:12, 14.
92.   43/xxii 452.

ing only bare rock. Historian Phillip Myers in his history textbook, *General History for Colleges and High Schools*, writes, "Alexander the Great reduced Tyre to ruins in 332 BC. Tyre recovered in a measure from this blow, but never regained the place she had previously held in the world. The larger part of the site of the once great city is now as bare as the top of a rock—a place where the fishermen that still frequent the spot spread their nets to dry."[93]

Wow, this was dramatic stuff—I had no idea...

The City of Samaria

The prophets Hosea (748–690 BC) and Micah (738–690 BC) each predicted the destruction of Samaria, the capital city of the Northern Kingdom of Israel. Not only did these prophets predict violence and destruction, but they declared that this great city would become "as a heap in the field," with its stones poured down into the valley, and vineyards planted in place of its great walls, with even the foundations being removed.[94]

History tells us that Sargon took Samaria by the sword in 722 BC. Later, Alexander took the city violently in 331 BC, as did Hyrcanus in 120 BC. What's remarkable is not the violent demise of Samaria and its people, but rather, some of the historic specifics of what then happened to that once great city.

Reactions upon visiting the ancient spot have been recorded for centuries. In 1697, Henry Maundrell declared: "This great city is now wholly converted into gardens, and all the tokens that remain to testify that there has ever been such a place, are only on the north side..." Floyd Hamilton continues: "To-day the top of the hill where Samaria stood is a cultivated field with the foundations of the columns marking the place where the palaces and mansions stood. At the foot of the hill, in the valley, lie the foundation stones of the city..."[95] Finally, from Van de Velde:

> *Her foundations discovered, her streets ploughed up, and covered with corn fields and olive gardens...Samaria has been destroyed, but her rubbish has been thrown down into the valley; her foundation stones, those grayish ancient quadrangular*

---

93. Phillip Myers, *General History for Colleges and High Schools*, Boston, Ginn & Co., 2003, 55.
94. Hosea 13:16 and Micah 1:6.
95. McDowell, *Evidence that Demands a Verdict*, vol. 1, 282.

stones of the time of Omri and Ahab, are discovered, and lie scattered about on the slope of the hill.[96]

I read prophecy after prophecy…

I read them closely and let them sink in…

I took notes and collected excerpts and articles…

I was fascinated with the probabilities…

In his classic book, *Science Speaks*, Peter Stoner reviews some of the historical prophecies of the Old Testament, including Babylon, Tyre, Samaria, Gaza-Ashkelon, Jerusalem, Palestine, Moab-Ammon, and Petra-Edom. Stoner uses peer-reviewed mathematical analysis and principles of probability to conclude:

> *No human being has ever made predictions which hold any comparison to those we have considered, and had them accurately come true. The span of time between the writing of these prophecies and their fulfillment is so great that the most severe critic cannot claim that the predictions were made after the events happened.*[97]

For me, these historical prophecies weren't a tabloid lark…They weren't a contrivance…They weren't an after-the-fact hoax…They were absolutely legitimate.

As I reviewed my notes, I was truly excited, yet somehow uneasy…

As I studied these prophecies, I couldn't deny a recurring theme in the Old Testament…

Who was this predicted "Messiah" (Shiloh) mentioned as far back as the Book of Genesis?[98]

Who was this coming "Ruler" that the prophet Micah said would be born in Bethlehem, yet preexisted time itself?[99]

---

96. Ibid., 283.
97. Peter Stoner, *Science Speaks: An Evaluation of Certain Christian Evidences*, Moody Press, 1963, 115. http://www.geocities.com/stonerdon/science_speaks.html#c8.
98. Genesis 49:10.
99. Micah 5:2.

Who was this "Immanuel" (literally, "God-with-us") who the prophet Isaiah declared would be born of a virgin?[100]

Who was this "Redeemer" that Job said would come to save him and the world from death?[101]

Who was this prophesied "Son" that would be referred to as "Wonderful," "Counselor," "Mighty God," and the "Prince of Peace?"[102]

For me, the biblical test of prophecy came through! Intellectually, I had no choice but to accept the facts—the fulfilled prophecies of the Old Testament authenticate its inspiration from outside our time dimension. There was no other logical conclusion…as hard as I tried to find one!

But what about all those predictions of a coming Jewish "Messiah" (Savior) found throughout a number of books in the Old Testament? What was I to make of them? Did I really need to deal with those as part of my prophecy analysis?

I was so uneasy with what the Old Testament was revealing to me that I went out and purchased an English version of the Hebrew Tanakh. I figured that some of these predictions had to be after-the-fact insertions by non-Jews. I decided to go "right to the source" and clear this up…

Guess what? The same "Messianic" predictions were there in the Jewish Scriptures—plain as day…

My heart was truly uneasy…I needed to slow myself down…I needed to retreat to my intellect again…

I went back to my original list of questions and issues in my notebook…

Contradictions in the Bible

OK, prophecy aside, what about all those contradictions and inaccuracies in the Bible? If this is some kind of special book from God, how can I reconcile an imperfect Bible with a supposedly perfect source?

---

100. Isaiah 7:14.
101. Job 19:25.
102. Isaiah 9:6.

The alleged inaccuracies and errors in today's Bible translations were a major intellectual barrier for me—so I decided to dive into that argument for awhile...When I started this journey, I hadn't read much of the Bible yet. However, I still maintained a "list" of Bible contradictions to help substantiate why I totally rejected it! It was time for me to pull out that list again...

To be fair, I knew I needed to analyze my list of alleged Bible errors according to traditional rules of logic and reason. Like many things in life, certain facts can appear contradictory, but further investigation reveals something different. "The Law of Non-Contradiction," which is the basis of all logical reasoning, maintains that something cannot be "*a*" and "*non-a*" at the same time. For instance, it can't be day and night at the same time and at the same place. Therefore, if a biblical scripture violates this Law, it has been established as a contradiction. However, based on the same Law, two statements can differ without being in contradiction.

For example, one witness in a court case might testify that he saw two people at a crime scene, Jake and Sam, while another witness may only testify to seeing Sam. These statements are not contradictory. In fact, in a court of law, these statements could be considered complementary.

I quickly discovered that this is the nature of many of the alleged contradictions in the Bible. For instance, in Matthew, we read that Jesus met two blind men. In Mark and Luke, we read about Jesus meeting only one blind man.[103] In Matthew and Mark, we read that Jesus went to pray alone three times in the Garden of Gethsemane, whereas, in Luke, we read that Jesus went alone to pray on one occasion.[104] Under legal rules of evidence and the Law of Non-Contradiction, these aren't contradictory scriptures, and yet they made my list.

Some Bible contradictions appear contradictory solely because of the intricacies of Bible translation. Analysis of the original languages of the Bible (Hebrew for the Old Testament and Greek for the New Testament) can solve many apparent issues. It's no different than any other textual review of translated material. All languages (including especially Hebrew and Greek) have special limitations and nuances that cause difficulty in translation. The historical context of the translation can also cause some misunderstanding.

---

103. Matthew 9:27-31; Mark 8:22-26 and Luke 18:35-43.
104. Matthew 26:36-46 and Mark 14:32-42; Luke 22:39-46.

For instance, the Book of Acts has two accounts of Paul's conversion on the Road to Damascus. In Acts 9:7: "...*the men which journeyed with him stood speechless, hearing a voice, but seeing no man.*" In Acts 22:9: "...*they that were with me saw indeed the light, and were afraid; but they heard not the voice of him that spake to me*" (King James Version). At first glance, these accounts seem contradictory—one says that Paul's companions heard a voice, while the other says that no voice was heard. However, the Greek text solves the matter. "The construction of the verb 'to hear' (*akouo*) is not the same in both accounts. In Acts 9:7 it's used with the genitive, in Acts 22:9 with the accusative. The construction with the genitive simply expresses that something is being heard or that certain sounds reach the ear; nothing is indicated as to whether a person understands what he hears or not. The construction with the accusative, however, describes a hearing, which includes mental apprehension of the message spoken. From this it becomes evident that the two passages are not contradictory."[105] Therefore, Acts 22:9 doesn't deny that Paul's companions heard certain sounds; it simply says that they didn't understand the sounds that they heard.

As I continued to pick apart my list, I was actually embarrassed with myself. Sure, there are a few inconsequential names and numbers in the Bible that must be considered copyist errors that arose over thousands of years. However, I was able to logically explain every alleged inconsistency of any real significance on my list.

I hadn't even checked this stuff out! I called myself an intellectual skeptic, and yet I hadn't treated this matter with much credibility. Sadly, I had rejected the Bible by focusing on a little list of alleged contradictions. Yet, when presented with the miracle of the Bible's structure, survival, integration, historical veracity, archaeological evidence, scientific insights, outside corroborating records, and hundreds of fulfilled prophecies, I stubbornly looked the other way. Now, the double standard I was living started to reveal itself to me!

◆   ◆   ◆

I actually stopped reading (or even thinking) for about a week...

I had no where else to go...

---

105. W.F. Arndt, *Does the Bible Contradict Itself?*, 13-14.

What was I going to do with all of these new realities in my life...?

What was I going to do with those Old Testament prophecies of a coming Messiah...?

FURTHER STUDY SUGGESTIONS—PART II

Various editors, **Zondervan Handbook to the Bible**, Zondervan Publishing House, 1999 (rev).

A credible and meticulous companion to reading the Bible, which presents the history, geography and culture of the biblical accounts. Full of maps, charts, pictures and illustrations, this handbook sheds light on certain leaders, battles, empires, etc.

Henry H. Halley, **Halley's Bible Handbook**, Zondervan Publishing House, 2000 (rev).

Another great Bible handbook full of maps, charts, photographs, history and archaeology.

Blue Letter Bible: Online Bible Search & Commentary Tool, http://www.blueletterbible.org/

Alfred J. Hoerth, **Archaeology and the Old Testament**, Baker Books, 1998 (updated 1999).

Dr. Hoerth is very careful to declare archaeology as dramatic confirmation of biblical history, but he downplays the tendency to use archaeological evidence to support theological beliefs. Throughout his research, he recognizes a clear separation between historical evidence and "theological proof" (p. 20). I found this to be a very credible and unbiased approach to starting a review of biblical people, places and events.

John McRay, **Archaeology and the New Testament**, Baker Books, 1991 (updated 2003).

Dr. McRay presents the architecture, society and religion of the first century Roman Empire, from the structures of Herod the Great to the City of Jerusalem. Through ancient cities, stones and manuscript fragments, we see the historical foundation for the biblical accounts of the New Testament.

Randall Price, **The Stones Cry Out: What Archaeology Reveals About the Truth of the Bible**, Harvest House Publishers, 1997.

Dr. Price presents the latest archaeological finds that shed light on events such as the early Israelites entering Canaan, the fall of Jericho, the Ark of the Covenant, the kings and prophets of Israel, the Assyrian and Babylonian invasions, the Dead Sea Scrolls, and the historical foundation of Jesus.

Biblical Archaeology Review, a monthly publication of the Biblical Archaeology Society.

This BAR publication presents academic articles in an easy-to-read general circulation magazine. http://www.biblicalarchaeology.org/

Paul Barnett, **Is the New Testament Reliable? A Look at the Historical Evidence**, Intervarsity Press, 1986.

A clear and straightforward book that tackles the following: How accurate is the historical information in the New Testament? Were any of the writers eyewitnesses to the events? Is the New Testament a myth? How biased were the writings of first century Christians? Is there any information on biblical events outside the Bible? When were the New Testament accounts written? Were errors introduced as manuscripts were copied over hundreds of years?

F.F. Bruce, **The New Testament Documents: Are They Reliable?** Intervarsity Press, 1943.

A classic and scholarly look at the questions addressed by Barnett's book.

Josh McDowell, **The New Evidence that Demands a Verdict**, Thomas Nelson Publishers, 1999.

A broad look at the Bible and its historical credibility. This book presents the latest in research and documentation regarding the manuscripts, archaeology, history and culture of the early Christian church and its foundation.

PART III
THE REALITY OF JESUS

The Jesus of History

Jesus Christ has been called many things by many people, including a great man, a great teacher, and a great prophet. There's really no legitimate scholar today that denies that Jesus is a historic figure that walked on this earth about 2,000 years ago, that he did remarkable wonders and acts of charity, and that he died a horrible death on a Roman cross just outside Jerusalem. Like these "scholars", I guess I never had a problem with this "historical Jesus." Similar to Buddha, Confucius, Zoroaster or Muhammad, I viewed Jesus as just another profound religious leader in history.

I must say, as a "practicing atheist," I experienced a number of people that totally rejected Jesus as an historic figure. They staunchly defended their various myth and conspiracy theories. However, I found their arguments to be very weak. Come on, the entire English-speaking world divides history into two principle periods: BC ("Before Christ") and AD ("Anno Domini"—Latin for "Year of Our Lord"). Whether one subscribes to the BC/AD labels or the new "politically correct" BCE/CE ("Common Era") labels, the birth of Jesus Christ has always been the dividing line in history.

Also, nobody can deny the fact that every leader of every major world religion has confronted the historic person of Jesus. Muslims recognize Jesus as a prophet, while Jews either see him as a blaspheming rebel or an exceptional rabbi elevated to deity by idolatrous Gentiles. Many Buddhists regard Jesus as a "bodhisattva" (a perfectly enlightened being who vows to help others), while there's a Hindu tradition that Jesus was actually a guru who learned yogic meditation in India.[1]

OK, so the person known as Jesus of Nazareth was an historic figure. Again, I really didn't have a problem with that reality. But what about his life and death as recorded in the Bible? Oh, wait…what about all those Old Testament prophecies of a coming Messiah ("Christos" in Greek)…?

---

1.   Kenneth L. Woodward, "The Other Jesus," *Newsweek*, March 27th, 2000.

Prophecies of a Coming Messiah

Messianic prophecy is the collection of over 300 predictions in the Jewish Scriptures about the future Messiah (Savior) of the Jewish people and the world. These predictions were written by multiple authors, in numerous books, over approximately 1,000 years.

Although I was now viewing the Bible as a credible source, and I was stunned by some of the historical prophecies I examined in the Old Testament, I just couldn't get over the gap dividing the Old Testament predictions from the New Testament Jesus. It was just too convenient...Or maybe it was just too perfect...I had to check them out and test them for myself...

I started reading and collecting the actual scriptures. I laid out the Old Testament passages and searched for the corresponding New Testament texts. As my little notebook took shape, it was really powerful! The Messiah had to fulfill all of these—not just some of them...The statistical odds started revealing themselves to me...I must say, I was totally baffled...

> Jesus said to them, "This is what I told you while I was still with you: **Everything must be fulfilled that is written about me in the Law of Moses, the Prophets and the Psalms.**"[2]

Here's a brief snapshot of a few prophecies I looked at during my notebook exercise...

- He would be born of a virgin (Isaiah 7:14/Matthew 1:21-23; Luke 1:26-35)
- He would be born in Bethlehem (Micah 5:2/Matthew 2:1; Luke 2:4-7)
- He would be heralded by a messenger of the Lord (John the Baptist) (Isaiah 40:3-5; Malachi 3:1/Matthew 3:1-3; 11:10; Mark 1:2-3; Luke 7:27)
- He would perform miracles (Isaiah 35:5-6; Matthew 9:35, and throughout the gospels)
- He would preach good news (Isaiah 61:1-2/Luke 4:14-21)

---

2.   Luke 24:44 (NIV); emphasis mine.

- He would first present himself as king 173,880 days from the decree to rebuild Jerusalem (Daniel 9:25/Matthew 21:4-9; Mark 11:1-10; Luke 19:29-38)

- He would enter Jerusalem as king riding a donkey (Zechariah 9:9/Matthew 21:4-9; Mark 11:1-10; Luke 19:29-38)

- He would die a humiliating and painful death (Psalm 22; Isaiah 53/Matthew 27; Mark 15; Luke 23; John 19)

- His hands and feet would be pierced (Psalm 22:16;/Crucifixion accounts of Matthew 27; Mark 15; Luke 23; John 19)

- His executioners would cast lots for his clothing (Psalm 22:18; John 19:23-24)

- None of his bones would be broken in his execution (Psalm 34:20; John 19:32-36)

- His side would be pierced (Zechariah 12:10; John 19:34-37)

- He would die with the wicked and be buried in a rich man's tomb (Isaiah 53:9; Matthew 27:57-60)

Although some of the other predictions I looked at could be called "generalized," taken as a whole, these were remarkable to me! I couldn't get over the odds of just one man fulfilling each and every one of these predictions! Even when I tossed out a few of the more "basic" ones, I was still absolutely stunned by the statistical impossibility.

So, was the Jesus of the New Testament really the promised Messiah of the Old Testament? For me, I started to see the mathematical impossibility of just one man—Jesus—accidentally fulfilling or purposefully manipulating over 300 predictions written hundreds of years before his birth.

Professor Peter Stoner (1888–1980) discovered the same thing. Stoner was Chairman of the Departments of Mathematics and Astronomy at Pasadena City College until 1953, and Chairman of the Science Division of Westmont College from 1953 to 1957. Stoner calculated the probability of one man fulfilling only a handful of the over 300 Messianic prophecies. In 1944, he published his research results in *Science Speaks: Scientific Proof of the Accuracy of Prophecy and the Bible.* Stoner concluded that the probability of one person fulfilling just eight of the specific prophecies was one chance in 10^{17} (one followed by 17 zeros). How about one person fulfilling just 48 of the over 300 prophecies? Stoner calculated these odds at one chance in 10^{157}—way beyond statistical impossibility![3]

OK, this can't be considered true statistical science…Can it?

Actually, the American Scientific Affiliation gave Stoner's work their stamp of approval:

> *The manuscript for Science Speaks has been carefully reviewed by a committee of the American Scientific Affiliation members and by the Executive Council of the same group and has been found, in general, to be dependable and accurate in regard to the scientific material presented. The mathematical analysis included is based upon principles of probability which are thoroughly sound and Professor Stoner has applied these principles in a proper and convincing way.*[4]

I was blown away! I had never really looked at this stuff. I had never really thought it all through…

I mean, this wasn't generalized stuff!

The Book of Daniel was written 500 years before the birth of Jesus. In Chapter 9, Daniel predicts the very day that the Messiah would enter Jerusalem and present himself as king for the first time. The prophecy states that 69 weeks of years (69 x 7 = 483 years) would pass from the decree to rebuild Jerusalem until the coming of the Messiah.[5] Since Daniel was written in Babylon during the Jewish captivity after the fall of Jerusalem, this prophecy was based on the Babylonian 360-day calendar. Thus, 483 years x 360 days = 173,880 days.

According to records found in the Shushan (Susa) Palace, and confirmed in Nehemiah 2:1, the decree to rebuild Jerusalem was issued by the Persian king, Artaxerxes Longimanus, on March 5, 444 BC. Remarkably, 173,880 days later (adjusting for leap years), on March 30, 33 AD, Jesus rode into Jerusalem on a

---

3.   Peter Stoner, *Science Speaks: Scientific Proof of the Accuracy of Prophecy and the Bible*, 1944, 109-10.

4.   American Scientific Affiliation, H. Harold Hartzler, Ph.D., Secretary-Treasurer, Goshen College, Ind. (Peter Stoner, *Science Speaks: Scientific Proof of the Accuracy of Prophecy and the Bible*, 1944, Foreword).

5.   Daniel 9:25.

donkey (fulfilling the prophecy in Zechariah 9:9).[6] Five days later, Jesus was crucified on a Roman cross just outside Jerusalem. (Actually, the form of his execution and even his last words were foretold hundreds of years earlier in Psalm 22.) Three days later, the New Testament accounts declare that Jesus rose from the dead on Easter Sunday, fulfilling numerous other prophecies of the long-awaited Messiah.

I stopped myself...

OK, that's all terrific stuff, but something was holding me back...I needed more...I needed something to squash my nagging doubt...Where's the evidence that these Messianic prophecies weren't written after the death of Jesus by a group of zealots that wanted to deify their departed religious leader...? I needed something else—I needed one more piece of evidence that showed these predictions were in black and white prior to the time of Jesus...

And there it was...

The Dead Sea Scrolls

The Dead Sea Scrolls have been called the greatest manuscript discovery of modern times. They were discovered between 1947 and 1956 in eleven caves along the northwest shore of the Dead Sea. This is an arid region 13 miles east of Jerusalem and 1,300 feet below sea level. The Dead Sea Scrolls are comprised of the remains of approximately 825 to 870 separate scrolls, represented by tens of thousands of fragments. The texts are most commonly made of animal skins, but also papyrus and one of copper. Most of the texts are written in Hebrew and Aramaic, with a few in Greek.

The Dead Sea Scrolls appear to be the library of a Jewish sect, considered most likely the Essenes. Near the caves are the ancient ruins of Qumran, a village excavated in the early 1950's that shows connections to both the Essenes and the scrolls. The Essenes were strictly observant Jewish scribes. The library appears to have been hidden away in caves around the outbreak of the First Jewish Revolt (66–70 AD) as the Roman army advanced against the Jews.

---

6. Some great scholars will argue these dates within a few days or up to a year, but this prophecy is still staggering in scope. See, Sir Robert Anderson, *The Coming Prince*, Kregel Classics, 1957 reprint, 127-128, 221.

The Dead Sea Scrolls can be divided into two categories—biblical and non-biblical. Fragments of every book of the Jewish Scriptures (Old Testament) have been discovered, except for the book of Esther. Now identified among the scrolls are 19 fragments of Isaiah, 25 fragments of Deuteronomy and 30 fragments of the Psalms. The virtually intact Isaiah Scroll, which contains some of the most dramatic Messianic prophecy, is 1,000 years older than any previously known manuscript of Isaiah.

Based on various dating methods, including paleographic, scribal, and carbon-14, the Dead Sea Scrolls were written during the period from about 200 B.C. to 68 AD. Many crucial Messianic manuscripts (such as Psalm 22, Isaiah 53 and Isaiah 61) date to at least 100 BC. As such, the Dead Sea Scrolls have revolutionized textual criticism of the Old Testament and Messianic prophecy. Phenomenally, the biblical texts of Qumran are in substantial agreement with the Masoretic text, Septuagint, and variant translations of the Old Testament we use today.[7]

Wow, what a find! Until recently (in historic terms), the extra piece of evidence I "needed" didn't exist. Now, it does! We now have dramatic evidence that the key Messianic prophecies contained in today's Old Testament are the same Messianic prophecies that existed prior to the time Jesus walked this earth. There was no contrivance after-the-fact...There was no conspiracy...Simply, Jesus fulfilled the requirements of the Jewish Messiah!

My study of archaeology had gone full circle...The Dead Sea Scrolls sat untouched in a perfect, arid environment for approximately 2,000 years. In 1947, a Bedouin shepherd stumbles upon arguably the most important archaeological find in history. Then, one year later, against tremendous odds, the Jewish people return to their homeland as a formal nation for the first time since 70 AD, fulfilling a number of major historical prophecies.[8]

Wow, I really felt a sense of wonder!

We really live in a remarkable time in history...

---

7.   See Price, *Secrets of the Dead Sea Scrolls*, 1996; Eisenman & Wise, *The Dead Sea Scrolls Uncovered*, 1994; Golb, *Who Wrote the Dead Sea Scrolls?*, 1995; Wise, Abegg & Cook, *The Dead Sea Scrolls, A New Translation*, 1999.
8.   See, for example, Isaiah 11:11-12, Ezekiel 37:21-23, and Jeremiah 23:7-8.

For me, I now had the utmost confidence that the Old Testament that we read today is substantially the same as existed before the birth of Jesus. This means that the over 300 Old Testament prophecies of the coming Messiah were in black-and-white before the New Testament writers were even on the scene.

Wait, Is this Circular Reasoning?

Stop. I spotted another potential issue here…I've just established that the Old Testament predictions of a coming Messiah pre-existed Jesus, but the only thing telling me that Jesus was the person who fulfilled these predictions is the New Testament. Therefore, I have one religious book being used to support the prophecies in another religious book—the New Testament accounts to document Old Testament prophetic fulfillment. Isn't this circular reasoning? Aren't we using the Bible to validate the Bible?

I went back and looked at my notes regarding the Bible…I was reminded that the Bible is often viewed as one book, and therefore, criticized on the basis of self-fulfilling integrity. However, the Bible is comprised of 66 separate and distinct texts written by some 40 authors who often had nothing to do with each other. If we view each text on its own, the level of validity and corroboration within the biblical volume itself is remarkable. The Bible actually validates itself through the inherent design that bonds its 66 separate books together in one integrative work.

When objectively analyzed, why should we have a problem using the 27 New Testament texts to help validate the 39 Old Testament texts? We're merely using one collection of ancient historical documents to establish the veracity of another collection of ancient historical documents…Academic historians do this all the time…

I stopped myself again.

I grasped this concept with respect to the 39 books of the Old Testament, where hundreds of years separated the authors and texts. However, since the 27 books of the New Testament were put together in a fairly short period of time, maybe they were more apt to be contrived as a whole by a tightly connected group of conspiring zealots. What about that? Are there any corroborating sources outside this tight-knit religious group?

Then I remembered my initial study of Tacitus (see part two) and recalled that other writers recorded "biblical" events outside the Bible...

Therefore, although I was well on my way to deflating the "circular reasoning" argument regarding the Bible, I realized I could avoid the issue altogether by returning to the "extra-biblical" historical documentation of Old Testament prophetic fulfillment.

For example, is there any documentation outside the New Testament that shows that Jesus was executed as predicted in Jewish Scriptures such as Psalm 22 and Isaiah 53?

Guess what? There is...

Corroborating Sources Outside the Bible

I soon discovered there are numerous Non-Christian sources outside the biblical texts that corroborate the events of the New Testament. In fact, there are a variety of extra-biblical sources that directly mention Jesus Christ and the rise of Christianity. I found this stunning! How could I discredit sources of historical evidence that weren't sympathetic to the person of Jesus or the cause of Christianity? In law, a witness that's either indifferent or antagonistic to the matter in question can be the most powerful testimony available.

I was more than intrigued. I started checking out some of these early, disinterested sources...

I started with the historian Tacitus, since I had just read his small yet powerful piece on Pontius Pilate and Christus (Christ)...

Cornelius Tacitus (c. 55–120 AD) was considered a great historian of ancient Rome. His masterpiece, *Annals*, is represented by a two-volume set (chapters 1-6, with one surviving manuscript; and chapters 11-16, known as *Historiae*, with 32 surviving manuscripts).[9]

As background, on July 19, 64 AD, a fire started in Rome that burned for nine days, finally destroying nearly three-quarters of the city. According to Tacitus,

---

9.   One credible translation of these two surviving chapter sets is available at MIT's website: http://classics.mit.edu/Tacitus/annals.html.

rumors spread that the fire was planned by the wickedly unstable Emperor Nero himself. In response, Nero created a diversion by calling for the torture and execution of Christians.

> *Consequently, to get rid of the report, Nero fastened the guilt and inflicted the most exquisite tortures on a class hated for their abominations, called Christians by the populace. Christus, from whom the name had its origin, suffered the extreme penalty during the reign of Tiberius at the hands of one of our procurators, Pontius Pilatus, and a most mischievous superstition, thus checked for the moment, again broke out not only in Judaea, the first source of the evil, but even in Rome, where all things hideous and shameful from every part of the world find their centre and become popular. Accordingly, an arrest was first made of all who pleaded guilty; then, upon their information, an immense multitude was convicted, not so much of the crime of firing the city, as of hatred against mankind. Mockery of every sort was added to their deaths. Covered with the skins of beasts, they were torn by dogs and perished, or were nailed to crosses, or were doomed to the flames and burnt, to serve as a nightly illumination, when daylight had expired.*
>
> *Nero offered his gardens for the spectacle, and was exhibiting a show in the circus, while he mingled with the people in the dress of a charioteer or stood aloft on a car. Hence, even for criminals who deserved extreme and exemplary punishment, there arose a feeling of compassion; for it was not, as it seemed, for the public good, but to glut one man's cruelty, that they were being destroyed.*[10]

From Tacitus, probably the leading Roman historian of the period, there's no doubt that Christians existed in 64 AD. In addition, they faced hideous persecution for their belief in Christ, a true historical figure who was executed in Judaea during the reign of Tiberius at the hands of Pontius Pilate.

Flavius Josephus (37–100 AD), a Jewish general and member of the priestly aristocracy of the Jews, turned to the side of the Roman Empire in the great Jewish revolt of 66–70 AD. Josephus spent the rest of his life in or around Rome as an advisor and historian to three emperors, Vespasian, Titus and Domitian. For centuries, the works of Josephus were more widely read in Europe than any book other than the Bible. They are invaluable sources of eyewitness testimony to the development of Western civilization, including the foundation and growth of Christianity in the 1st Century.

Remarkably, Josephus mentions New Testament events and people in some of his works. For me, this was some of the most significant evidence against the leg-

---

10.   Tacitus, *Annales, Historiae*, Chapter 15, paragraphs 54 and 55.

end theories that plagued my view of early Christianity. Here are some excerpts I found fascinating:

> *At this time there was a wise man who was called Jesus. And his conduct was good, and he was known to be virtuous. And many people from among the Jews and other nations became his disciples. Pilate condemned him to be crucified and to die. And those who had become his disciples did not abandon his discipleship. They reported that he had appeared to them three days after his crucifixion and that he was alive; accordingly, he was perhaps the Messiah concerning whom the prophets have recounted wonders.*[11]

***

> *After the death of the procurator Festus, when Albinus was about to succeed him, the high-priest Ananius considered it a favorable opportunity to assemble the San-hedrin. He therefore caused James the brother of Jesus, who was called Christ, and several others, to appear before this hastily assembled council, and pronounced upon them the sentence of death by stoning. All the wise men and strict observers of the law who were at Jerusalem expressed their disapprobation of this act...Some even went to Albinus himself, who had departed to Alexandria, to bring this breach of the law under his observation, and to inform him that Ananius had acted illegally in assembling the Sanhedrin without the Roman authority.*[12]

***

> *Now some of the Jews thought that the destruction of Herod's army came from God, and that very justly, as a punishment of what he did against John, that was called the Baptist: for Herod slew him, who was a good man, and commanded the Jews to exercise virtue, both as to righteousness towards one another, and piety towards God, and so to come to baptism; for that the washing [with water] would be acceptable to him, if they made use of it, not in order to the putting away [or the*

---

11. *Antiquities*, Book 18, chapter 3, paragraph 3 (translated from 4th century Arabic manuscript). An even more phenomenal Greek version of this text exists, which many scholars declare was "doctored" a bit in a few places. However, this version was quoted as early as 325 AD:

> *Now there was about this time Jesus, a wise man, if it be lawful to call him a man; for he was a doer of wonderful works, a teacher of such men as receive the truth with pleasure. He drew over to him both many of the Jews and many of the Gentiles. He was [the] Christ. And when Pilate, at the suggestion of the principal men amongst us, had condemned him to the cross, those that loved him at the first did not forsake him; for he appeared to them alive again the third day; as the divine prophets had foretold these and ten thousand other wonderful things concerning him. And the tribe of Christians, so named from him, are not extinct at this day.*

12. *Antiquities*, Book 20, chapter 9, paragraph 1.

remission] of some sins [only], but for the purification of the body; supposing still that the soul was thoroughly purified beforehand by righteousness.[13]

These three quotes from Josephus really speak for themselves! Professor Shlomo Pines, a well known Israeli scholar, discusses the fact of Jesus' historicity and the references to Jesus by Josephus:

> *In fact, as far as probabilities go, no believing Christian could have produced such a neutral text: for him the only significant point about it could have been its attesting the historical evidence of Jesus. But the fact is that until modern times this particular hare (i.e. claiming Jesus is a hoax) was never started. Even the most bitter opponents of Christianity never expressed any doubt as to Jesus having really lived.*[14]

Pliny the Younger (c. 62–c.113 AD) was the Roman Governor of Bithynia (present-day northwestern Turkey). Around 111 or 112 AD, he wrote the following letter to Emperor Trajan of Rome asking for advice on how to deal with Christians.

> *It is a rule, Sir, which I inviolably observe, to refer myself to you in all my doubts; for who is more capable of guiding my uncertainty or informing my ignorance? Having never been present at any trials of the Christians, I am unacquainted with the method and limits to be observed either in examining or punishing them. Whether any difference is to be allowed between the youngest and the adult; whether repentance admits to a pardon, or if a man has been once a Christian it avails him nothing to recant; whether the mere profession of Christianity, albeit without crimes, or only the crimes associated therewith are punishable—in all these points I am greatly doubtful.*

> *In the meanwhile, the method I have observed towards those who have denounced to me as Christians is this: I interrogated them whether they were Christians; if they confessed it I repeated the question twice again, adding the threat of capital punishment; if they still persevered, I ordered them to be executed. For whatever the nature of their creed might be, I could at least feel not doubt that contumacy and inflexible obstinacy deserved chastisement. There were others also possessed with the same infatuation, but being citizens of Rome, I directed them to be carried thither.*

---

13. *Antiquities*, Book 18, chapter 5, paragraph 2.
14. Shlomo Pines, *An Arabic Version of the Testamonium Flavianum and its Implications*, Jerusalem Academic Press, 1971, 69.
    See also, http://www.blueletterbible.org/Comm/mark_eastman/messiah/sfm_ap2.html#note6b.

These accusations spread (as is usually the case) from the mere fact of the matter being investigated and several forms of the mischief came to light. A placard was put up, without any signature, accusing a large number of persons by name. Those who denied they were, or had ever been, Christians, who repeated after me an invocation to the gods, and offered adoration, with wine and frankincense, to your image, which I had ordered to be brought for that purpose, together with those of the gods, and who finally cursed Christ—none of which acts, it is into performing—these I thought it proper to discharge. Others who were named by that informer at first confessed themselves Christians, and then denied it; true, they had been of that persuasion but they had quitted it, some three years, others many years, and a few as much as twenty-five years ago. They all worshipped your statue and the images of the gods, and cursed Christ.

They affirmed, however, the whole of their guilt, or their error, was, that they were in the habit of meeting on a certain fixed day before it was light, when they sang in alternate verses a hymn to Christ, as to a god, and bound themselves by a solemn oath, not to any wicked deeds, but never to commit any fraud, theft, or adultery, never to falsify their word, nor deny a trust when they should be called upon to deliver it up; after which it was their custom to separate, and then reassemble to partake of food—but food of an ordinary and innocent kind. Even this practice, however, they had abandoned after the publication of my edict, by which, according to your orders, I had forbidden political associations. I judged it so much the more necessary to extract the real truth, with the assistance of torture, from two female slaves, who were styled deaconesses: but I could discover nothing more than depraved and excessive superstition.

I therefore adjourned the proceedings, and betook myself at once to your counsel. For the matter seemed to me well worth referring to you, especially considering the numbers endangered. Persons of all ranks and ages, and of both sexes are, and will be, involved in the prosecution. For this contagious superstition is not confined to the cities only, but has spread through the villages and rural districts; it seems possible, however, to check and cure it.[15]

This is quite a letter preserved from antiquity. I reproduced a great deal of it here, because it was so powerful for me in its entirety. It speaks of Christianity spreading throughout the Roman Empire and it addresses the procedure for persecuting followers out of this "superstition." It also mentions Christ by name three times as the center of Christianity and describes Christian practices, including the worship of Christ "as to a god."

---

15.   Plinius Secundus, *Epistles*, X.96.

Suetonius was a secretary and historian to Hadrian, Emperor of Rome from 117 to 138 AD. Regarding Emperor Claudius (41–54 AD) and the Riot of Rome in 49 AD, Suetonius wrote:

> *As the Jews were making constant disturbances at the instigation of Chrestus [Christ], he [Claudius] expelled them from Rome.*[16]

Interestingly, Acts 18:2 relates that Paul met Aquila and his wife Priscilla just after they left Italy because Claudius had expelled them.

Later, Suetonius wrote about the great fire of Rome in 64 AD:

> *Punishment by Nero was inflicted on the Christians, a class of men given to a new and mischievous superstition.*[17]

Mara Bar-Serapion, a stoic philosopher from Syria, wrote this letter to his son from prison sometime after 70 AD:

> *What advantage did the Athenians gain from putting Socrates to death? Famine and plague came upon them as a judgment for their crime. What advantage did the men of Samos gain from burning Pythagoras? In a moment their land was covered with sand. What advantage did the Jews gain from their executing their wise king? It was just after that that their kingdom was abolished. God justly avenged these three wise men: The Athenians died of hunger; the Samians were overwhelmed by the sea; the Jews, ruined and driven from their land, live in complete dispersion. But Socrates did not die for good; he lived on in the statue of Plato. Pythagoras did not die for good; he lived on in the statue of Hera. Nor did the wise king die for good; he lived on in the teaching which he had given.*[18]

This letter refers to Jesus as being the "wise king." The writer is obviously not a Christian because he places Jesus on an equal level with Socrates and Pythagoras. Without bias in his reference to Jesus and the church, this letter is a valuable historical reference regarding the historicity of Jesus.

---

16. Suetonius, *Life of Claudius*, 25.4. See also, McDowell, *New Evidence that Demands a Verdict*, 121-122.
17. Suetonius, *Lives of the Caesars*, 26.2. See also, Ibid.
18. British Museum Syriac Manuscript, Addition 14, 658. See also, Eastman & Smith, *The Search for Messiah*, 251-252.

Lucian of Samosata was a 2nd century Greek philosopher. This preserved text is obviously satirical, but it's a powerful extra-biblical source:

> *The Christians, you know, worship a man to this day—the distinguished person-age who introduced their novel rites, and was crucified on that account…You see, these misguided creatures started with the general conviction that they are immor-tal for all time, which explains the contempt of death and voluntary self-devotion which are so common among them; and then it was impressed them by their origi-nal lawgiver that they are all brothers, from the moment that they are converted, and deny the gods of Greece, and worship the crucified sage, and live after his laws. All this they take quite on faith, with the result that they despise all worldly goods alike, regarding them merely as common property.*[19]

This piece is unflattering at best, but it absolutely supports the person of Jesus Christ ("the crucified sage") and the survival of the Christian Church into the second century.

Ancient Rabbinical References to Y'shua (Jesus)

Of all the ancient sources for Jesus, the least favorably biased seem to be rabbinic in origin. There are actually a significant number of references to Jesus, but many of them use names like "that man" when they refer to Jesus Christ. Therefore, some of the references are now considered unreliable.

Regardless, in the Babylonian Talmud, the formal commentary on the Jewish Laws compiled between 200–500 AD, there's a powerful reference to Jesus:

> *It has been taught: On the Eve of the Passover, they hanged Yeshu. And an announcer went out in front of him, for forty days saying: 'he is going to be stoned because he practiced sorcery and enticed and led Israel astray.' Anyone who knows anything in his favor, let him come and plead in his behalf.' But, not having found anything in his favor, they hanged him on the Eve of the Passover.*[20]

This is considered to be a very credible Jewish reference to Jesus ("Yeshu"). Here, the rabbinical writers verify that Jesus was an historic figure, that he was crucified

---

19. Lucien of Samosata, "Death of Pelegrine," *The Works of Lucian of Samosata*, 4 vols. Trans. By H.W. Fowler and F.G. Fowler, Clarendon Press, 1949, 11-13.
20. Babylonian Talmud, Sanhedrin 43A.

on the eve of the Passover and that he did miracles, referred to as "sorcery." The events surrounding the life of Jesus were not denied, but definitely verified.

Well, I was looking for unbiased sources, outside the Bible, that speak to the person of Jesus, his death by capital punishment, and the rise of a religion in his name. Remarkably, that's exactly what I got!

The non-Christian historical accounts of Cornelius Tacitus, Flavius Josephus, Pliny the Younger, Suetonius, Mara Bar-Serapion, Lucan of Samosata, and even the writings of the extremely biased Jewish Sanhedrin all vindicate the Biblical accounts of the life and death of Jesus Christ in the first century AD.

In addition to the nine New Testament authors who wrote about Jesus in separate accounts, I found at least twenty additional early Christian authors, four heretical writings, and seven non-Christian sources that make explicit mention of Jesus in their writings within 150 years of his life. This amounts to a minimum of 40 authors, all of whom explicitly mention Jesus and the expansion of a spiritual movement in his name. More authors mention Jesus Christ within 150 years of his life than mention the Roman Emperor who reigned during His lifetime. Scholars are only aware of ten sources that mention Emperor Tiberius within 150 years of his life, including Luke, Tacitus, Suetonius, and Paterculus. Thus, within this short time frame, the number of ancient writers who mention Jesus outnumber those who mention the leader of the entire Roman Empire (effectively, the ancient world of the time) by a ratio of 4:1![21]

Alright, that's fantastic evidence for the historical life and death of a religious leader named Jesus Christ, but what about the rest?

What about the alleged miracles…?

What about the greatest miracle—his resurrection from the dead…?

Can a Rational Person Accept Miracles?

Actually, I jumped this hurdle pretty quick. For me, the suspension (or violation) of natural laws involved in biblical miracles is really no different than what we

---

21. See Josh McDowell, *The New Evidence that Demands a Verdict*, Thomas Nelson Publishers, 1999, 119-136. See also generally, Gary Habermas and Michael Licona, *The Case for the Resurrection of Jesus*, Kregel, 2004.

witness on a day-to-day basis. There are inherent natural forces represented by the laws of physics, chemical properties and mathematical formulae, and there are volitional forces that can interact or counteract the natural ones. For instance, the laws of gravity that hold a rock to the ground are not suspended (or violated) when a boy counteracts gravity by applying a greater physical force to pick up and throw the rock. The same logic holds when we read the eye-witness accounts of Jesus walking on water or turning water to wine. From a rational basis, he's merely applying a volitional force outside what we know as the natural laws within our four material dimensions.

I may be philosophically pre-disposed to dismiss any reference to supernatural events, but that doesn't mean they can't and don't occur. Given the caveat that there is a God, miracles are very reasonable. A supernatural agent is not logically constrained by the effects of his supernatural cause—thus God is not restricted by the naturalistic laws governing our universe. Natural law is God's creation, instituted by God to govern his creation. The creator is not boxed-in by his creation. When considering a supernatural agent, it's logical to "think outside of the box."

Given the reality of a supernatural creator, the gospel accounts of the miracles of Jesus are very reasonable. Some believe these texts were inspired by God himself. However, whether or not you personally hold them in such high esteem, at the very least the gospels represent four separate historical accounts written by four individual authors who, according to secular criteria, independently document historical events. A philosophical predisposition to disregard anything theological or miraculous is simply no reason to reject the gospel texts.

Again, let's consider the integrity of the gospels' writers, men willing to suffer intense persecution and even die in the defense of their individual testimonies. As I discussed previously, Luke is generally regarded as one of the greatest historians of antiquity. Dr. John McRay, professor of New Testament and Archaeology at Wheaton University in Illinois, pretty much sums it up:

> *The general consensus of both liberal and conservative scholars is that Luke is very accurate as a historian. He's erudite, he's eloquent, his Greek approaches classical quality, he writes as an educated man, and archaeological discoveries are showing over and over again that Luke is accurate in what he has to say.*[22]

---

22.   John McRay, quoted by Lee Strobel, *The Case For Christ*, Grand Rapids: Zondervan, 1998, 129.

Sir William Ramsey, one of the greatest archaeologists of modern times agrees, "Luke is a historian of the first rank."[23]

Have we any good reason to discard Luke's account of the life of Jesus?

How about the other gospel writers that gave their lives for their written testimonies?

What About the Resurrection?

OK, so here's the biggie…The core of the whole matter…

Did Jesus really rise from the dead, and why is this event so important…?

In a very simple nutshell, the New Testament is founded on Jesus Christ and the power of his resurrection. Since the foundation of biblical Christianity is Jesus Christ and his resurrection, then the historical veracity of his life, death and resurrection are tantamount. For as Paul declared in his letter to the Corinthians:

> *And if Christ has not been raised, our preaching is useless and so is your faith. More than that, we are then found to be false witnesses about God, for we have testified about God that he raised Christ from the dead.*[24]

As an analytical person trained in the law, I found that the only legitimate way to investigate the resurrection of Jesus was to test the historical evidence without presupposition or bias. Therefore, to be fair, I decided to judge the evidence like any other historical event.

Based on standard rules of evidence, consistent testimony from multiple credible witnesses would be considered the strongest form of evidence available to a litigant. Therefore, if I found such testimony present in credible accounts of the historical record, I would have satisfied a major evidentiary challenge under traditional rules.

In fact, I did find multiple eye-witness testimonies regarding the resurrection of Jesus. In his letter to the Corinthian church, Paul established the following:

---

23. Sir William Ramsey, *The Bearing of Recent Discovery on the Trustworthiness of the New Testament*, 1915, p. 222.
24. 1 Corinthians 15:14-15.

For what I received I passed on to you as of first importance: that Christ died for our sins according to the Scriptures, that he was buried, that he was raised on the third day according to the Scriptures, and that he appeared to Peter, and then to the Twelve. After that, he appeared to more than five hundred of the brothers at the same time, most of whom are still living, though some have fallen asleep.[25]

Manuscript studies indicate that this was a very early creed of the Christian faith, written within a few years after the death of Jesus Christ. Therefore, it's dramatic that Paul ends the passage with "most of whom are still living." Paul was inviting people to check out the facts. He wouldn't have included a statement like that if he was trying to hide something like a conspiracy, hoax, myth or legend.

The resurrection of Jesus was also declared in numerous other accounts, including the appearance of Jesus to Mary Magdalene,[26] to other women,[27] to Cleopas and his companion,[28] to eleven disciples and others,[29] to ten apostles and others (excluding Thomas),[30] to the apostles (including Thomas),[31] to seven apostles,[32] to the disciples,[33] and to the apostles on the Mount of Olives.[34]

For me, the ultimate test of credibility for these eye-witnesses was that many of them faced horrible deaths for their eye-witness testimony. As I've said before, this is really dramatic! These witnesses knew the truth! What could they possibly gain by dying for a known lie? The evidence speaks for itself, these weren't just religious faithful dying for a religious belief, these were followers of Jesus dying for an historic event—His resurrection that established him as the Christ, the Son of God.

Over time, I found the resurrection of Jesus Christ to be one of the most attested facts of all antiquity. After rising from the dead and before ascending back into heaven, Jesus was seen by hundreds of eyewitnesses, many of whom died unflinchingly for their testimony. Christ's earliest followers were willing to suffer

---

25. 1 Corinthians 15:3-6.
26. John 20:10-18.
27. Matthew 28:8-10.
28. Luke 24:13-32.
29. Luke 24:33-49.
30. John 20:19-23.
31. John 20:26-30.
32. John 21:1-14.
33. Matthew 28:16-20.
34. Luke 24:50-52 and Acts 1:4-9.

and die for their story.[35] This established fact attests to the sincerity of their faith and strongly rules out deception on their part. In fact, all but one of the New Testament's writers were executed for proclaiming and defending Christ's resurrection (John alone was spared, but forced into exile by the Roman Emperor Titus Flavius Domitianius).

Granted, martyrdom in itself is not unique—many throughout history have willingly died for their beliefs. What makes the disciples' martyrdom extraordinary to me is that these men were in a position to actually know whether or not what they were professing was true. You see, no one will knowingly suffer horribly and ultimately die a brutal death in order to defend something they know to be a lie. For example, the September 11th suicide hijackers may have sincerely believed in what they died for, but they certainly weren't in a position to know whether or not what they believed was true. They put their faith in religious traditions passed down to them over many generations.

In contrast, the New Testament's martyrs either saw what they claimed to see or they didn't; plain and simple. Either they interacted with the resurrected Jesus or they didn't. Dramatically, these men clung to their testimonies even to their brutal deaths at the hands of their persecutors, and this despite being given every chance to recant and knowing full well whether their testimony was true or false. Why would so many men knowingly die for a lie? They had nothing to gain for lying and obviously everything to lose.

In addition to the disciples experiencing what they claimed to be resurrection appearances, there were even a few skeptics who believed Jesus had appeared to them alive after the crucifixion. Most biblical scholars today agree that Paul was a skeptic and even a persecutor of the early Christian church prior to experiencing a post-resurrection appearance. Most scholars also agree that James was a skeptic prior to experiencing what he called a post-resurrection appearance.

Paul's experience caused him to immediately change from a nasty persecutor of Christianity to one of its most aggressive advocates. He claimed that this change came only after personally interacting with the resurrected Christ, and he willingly suffered and died for his testimony. [36]

---

35. Historical sources: Luke, Clement of Rome, Polycarp, Ignatius, Dionysius of Corinth, Tertullian, Origen.
36. Historical sources: Paul, Luke, Clement of Rome, Polycarp, Tertullian, Dionysius of Corinth, Origen.

And prior to Jesus' resurrection, his very own brother, James, was a skeptic.[37] His experience of a post resurrection appearance is reported within five years of Jesus' crucifixion.[38] After personally interacting with the risen Christ, James became a leader of the Christian church in Jerusalem.[39] James willingly died for his belief that Jesus was the Messiah who had died and rose again.[40]

I had to ask myself...Would someone who was willing to suffer and die a horrible death in defense of the Scriptures be guilty of corrupting those very same Scriptures? That's crazy! And if that person did corrupt the Scriptures (or even allowed them to be corrupted) that would mean he knowingly suffered and died for a lie!

It's just human nature...No one suffers and dies for a known lie! OK, maybe one lunatic, but not a whole group of eye-witnesses...!

Finally, I took a look at some of the academic scholarship. I was truly surprised to find that a large number of scholars today agree that Christ's tomb was found empty. Consider...

1. *The Jerusalem Factor*. Since Jesus was publicly executed and buried in Jerusalem, it would have been impossible for Christianity to begin in Jerusalem while the body was still in the tomb. Christ's enemies in the Jewish leadership and Roman government would only have to exhume the corpse and publicly display it for the hoax to be shattered.

2. *The Jewish Response*. Rather than point to an occupied tomb, the Jewish leadership accused Christ's disciples of stealing his body. Wouldn't this strategy seem to establish that there was, in fact, a missing body?[41]

3. *The Women's Testimony*. In all four Gospel accounts of the empty tomb, women are listed as the primary witnesses. This would be an odd invention, since in both Jewish and Roman cultures women were not esteemed and their testimony was not admissible.

---

37. Mark, John.
38. 1 Corinthians 15:7.
39. Paul, Luke.
40. Historical sources: Josephus, Hegesippus, Clement of Alexandria.
41. Historical sources: Matthew, Justin, Tertullian.

When you understand the role of women in first-century Jewish society, what's really extraordinary is that this empty tomb story should feature women as the discoverers of the empty tomb in the first place. Women were on a very low rung of the social ladder in first-century Palestine. There are old rabbinical sayings that said, 'Let the words of Law be burned rather than delivered to women' and 'blessed is he whose children are male, but woe to him whose children are female.' Women's testimony was regarded as so worthless that they weren't even allowed to serve as legal witnesses in a Jewish court of Law. In light of this, it's absolutely remarkable that the chief witnesses to the empty tomb are these women...Any later legendary account would have certainly portrayed male disciples as discovering the tomb—Peter or John, for example. The fact that women are the first witnesses to the empty tomb is most plausibly explained by the reality that—like it or not—they were the discoverers of the empty tomb! This shows that the Gospel writers faithfully recorded what happened, even if it was embarrassing. This bespeaks the historicity of this tradition rather than its legendary status.[42]

OK, if I'm a lawyer, and I'm viewing this evidence through legal goggles, what am I missing? Anything...? Surely, other analytical legal minds have weighed this evidence...

Again, I was truly stunned to find that great legal minds had already done this...

Check these guys out...

Simon Greenleaf (1783–1853) was one of the founders of Harvard Law School. He authored the authoritative three-volume text, *A Treatise on the Law of Evidence* (1842), which is still considered "the greatest single authority on evidence in the entire literature of legal procedure."[43] Greenleaf literally wrote the rules of evidence for the U.S. legal system. He was certainly a man who knew how to weigh the facts. He was an atheist until he accepted a challenge by his students to investigate the case for Christ's resurrection. After personally collecting and examining the evidence based on rules of evidence that he helped establish, Greenleaf became a Christian and wrote the classic, *Testimony of the Evangelists.*

Let [the Gospel's] testimony be sifted, as it were given in a court of justice on the side of the adverse party, the witness being subjected to a rigorous cross-examina-

---

42. Dr. William Lane Craig, quoted by Lee Strobel, *The Case For Christ*, Grand Rapids: Zondervan, 1998, 293.

43. Knott, *The Dictionary of American Biography*, back cover of *The Testimony of the Evangelists.*

tion. The result, it is confidently believed, will be an undoubting conviction of their integrity, ability, and truth.[44]

Sir Lionel Luckhoo (1914–1997) is considered one of the greatest lawyers in British history. He's recorded in the *Guinness Book of World Records* as the "World's Most Successful Advocate," with 245 consecutive murder acquittals. He was knighted by Queen Elizabeth II—twice. Luckhoo declared:

> *I humbly add I have spent more than 42 years as a defense trial lawyer appearing in many parts of the world and am still in active practice. I have been fortunate to secure a number of successes in jury trials and I say unequivocally the evidence for the Resurrection of Jesus Christ is so overwhelming that it compels acceptance by proof which leaves absolutely no room for doubt.*[45]

Lee Strobel was a Yale-educated, award-winning journalist at the Chicago Tribune. As an atheist, he decided to compile a legal case against Jesus Christ and prove him to be a fraud by the weight of the evidence. As Legal Editor of the Tribune, Strobel's area of expertise was courtroom analysis. To make his case against Christ, Strobel cross-examined a number of Christian authorities, recognized experts in their own fields of study (including PhD's from such prestigious academic centers as Cambridge, Princeton, and Brandeis). He conducted his examination with no religious bias, other than his predisposition to atheism.

Remarkably, after compiling and critically examining the evidence for himself, Strobel became a Christian. Stunned by his findings, he organized the evidence into a book entitled, *The Case for Christ*, which won the Gold Medallion Book Award for excellence. Strobel asks one thing of each reader—remain unbiased in your examination of the evidence. In the end, judge the evidence for yourself, acting as the lone juror in the case for Christ…[46]

As a "lone juror," I sat quiet in my chair…

As jurors often do in the jury room, I asked to return once again to a provoking piece of evidence…

---

44. Simon Greenleaf, *The Testimony of the Evangelists: The Gospels Examined by the Rules of Evidence*, Kregel Classics, 1995, Backcover.
45. Sir Lionel Luckhoo, *The Question Answered: Did Jesus Rise from the Dead?* Luckhoo Booklets, back page. http://www.hawaiichristiansonline.com/sir_lionel.html.
46. Lee Strobel, *The Case For Christ*, Grand Rapids: Zondervan, 1998, 18.

The Dramatic Testimony of Persecution & Death

Since this is so powerful for me, I want to reexamine the persecution and death that was such a dramatic part of early Christian history. Like me, any skeptic who holds to a notion that the resurrection of Jesus Christ was a man-made legend created after-the-fact by a group of religious zealots, should sincerely check out the legacy of martyrdom. Eleven of the 12 apostles, and many of the other early disciples, died for their adherence to this story. This is so spectacular, since they all witnessed the alleged events surrounding Jesus and his resurrection, and still went to their deaths defending them. Why is this spectacular, when many throughout history have died martyred deaths for a religious belief? Because people don't die for a lie. Look at human nature throughout history. No conspiracy can be maintained when life or liberty is at stake. Dying for a belief is one thing, but numerous eye-witnesses dying for a known lie is quite another.

OK, I guess I've made my point…

Here's an account of early Christian persecution, as compiled from numerous sources outside the Bible, the most-famous of which is Foxes' *Christian Martyrs of the World*:[47]

Around 34 A.D., one year after the crucifixion of Jesus, Stephen was thrown out of Jerusalem and stoned to death. Approximately 2,000 Christians suffered martyrdom in Jerusalem during this period. About 10 years later, James, the son of Zebedee and the elder brother of John, was killed when Herod Agrippa arrived as governor of Judea. Agrippa detested the Christian sect of Jews, and many early disciples were martyred under his rule, including Timon and Parmenas. Around 54 A.D., Philip, a disciple from Bethsaida, in Galilee, suffered martyrdom at Heliopolis, in Phrygia. He was scourged, thrown into prison, and afterwards crucified. About six years later, Matthew, the tax-collector from Nazareth who wrote one of the Gospels, was preaching in Ethiopia when he suffered martyrdom by the sword. James, the brother of Jesus, administered the early church in Jerusalem and was the author of a biblical text by his name. At age 94, he was beat and stoned, and finally had his brains bashed out with a fuller's club.

Matthias was the apostle who filled the vacant place of Judas. He was stoned at Jerusalem and then beheaded. Andrew was the brother of Peter who preached

---

47. John Foxe, *Foxe's Book of Martyrs*, Ed. by W. Grinton Berry, Reprinted by Fleming H. Revell, 1998.

throughout Asia. On his arrival at Edessa, he was arrested and crucified on a cross, the two ends of which were fixed transversely in the ground (this is where we get the term, St. Andrew's Cross). Mark was converted to Christianity by Peter, and then transcribed Peter's account of Jesus in his Gospel. Mark was dragged to pieces by the people of Alexandria in front of Serapis, their pagan idol. It appears Peter was condemned to death and crucified at Rome. Jerome holds that Peter was crucified upside down, at his own request, because he said he was unworthy to be crucified in the same manner as his Lord. Paul suffered in the first persecution under Nero. Paul's faith was so dramatic in the face of martyrdom, that the authorities removed him to a private place for execution by the sword.

In about 72 A.D., Jude, the brother of James who was commonly called Thaddeus, was crucified at Edessa. Bartholomew preached in several countries and translated the Gospel of Matthew into the language of India. He was cruelly beaten and then crucified by idolaters there. Thomas, called Didymus, preached in Parthia and India, where he was thrust through with a spear by a group of pagan priests. Luke was the author of the Gospel under his name. He traveled with Paul through various countries and is supposed to have been hanged on an olive tree by idolatrous priests in Greece. Barnabas, of Cyprus, was killed without many known facts in about 73 A.D. Simon, surnamed Zelotes, preached in Mauritania, Africa, and even in Britain, where he was crucified in about 74 A.D. John, the "beloved disciple," was the brother of James. From Ephesus he was ordered to Rome, where he was cast into a cauldron of boiling oil. He escaped by miracle, without injury. Domitian afterwards banished him to the Isle of Patmos, where John wrote the last book of the Bible, Revelation. He was the only apostle who escaped a violent death.

Christian persecution didn't slow the growth of the Christian faith during the first few centuries after Jesus. Even as its early leaders died horrible deaths, Christianity flourished throughout the Roman Empire. How can this historical record of martyrdom be viewed as anything but powerful evidence for the truth of the Christian faith—a faith grounded in historical events and eye-witness testimonies?

What is "Christian Faith" Anyway?

So, where am I with all this...? Where has this journey taken me, and how should it impact my life? I intellectually believe that certain things happened in history, but what does that really mean for my life today...?

What is belief? What is faith?

Although the Christian faith is not based purely on evidence, it is definitely supported by evidence. Faith is not about turning off the brain and merely relying on the heart, or squashing reason in favor of emotion. No, Christian faith is about seeking and knowing Jesus with all facets of the human character. It's not a "blind faith" as I once thought...It's a "calculated faith" based on a preponderance of the evidence. Well, I've collected the evidence, and I've put it on trial...After a number of months in the jury room, I have returned with my personal verdict...Jesus Christ is who he claims to be...the Son of God who came to this earth about 2,000 years ago to offer true and lasting hope for mankind.

OK, now what...? I intellectually believe, by a preponderance of the evidence, that God exists, that the Bible is true, and that Jesus is his Son...How does this affect me?

I love the metaphor of a chair...Find the chair closest to you. Look at it closely. Examine its design. Is it structurally sound? Is it sufficiently engineered? Will the materials chosen by the manufacturer support your weight?

Most likely, you picked a chair that you believe will support you. That's belief. You applied logic, knowledge and experience to make an informed intellectual decision.

Now sit in the chair...That's faith! At one point, intellectual assent only goes so far. True living requires that we put our beliefs into action. Intellectual belief without actionable faith is hollow and meaningless...

Have you ever heard about the guy who walked a tight rope across Niagra Falls? Many people watched him do it. To them he asked, "Do you believe I can walk a tight rope across the Falls?" They all replied, "Yes." They had already seen him do it.

Then he pushed a wheel barrow on a tight rope across Niagra Falls. When he completed the feat, he asked the onlookers, "Do you believe I can walk a tight rope across the Falls pushing a wheel barrow?" To that they replied unanimously, "Yes." Because they saw him do that too.

Finally, a buddy of the tight rope walker climbs into the wheel barrow and the tight rope walker pushes him across the Falls. Wow, what a daring feat! When they finished, the tight rope walker asked the crowd, "Do you believe I can walk a tight rope across the Falls pushing a wheel barrow with a person in it?" To that they exclaimed, "Yes!" For they were now believers in this guy's awesome abilities.

Then he looked at the crowd and asked, "Who's next?"

There you have it…Belief vs. Faith…!

Jesus Christ at the Core

Why has the name "Jesus Christ" caused more division, agitation and controversy than any other name in history?

Come on, why…?

If I bring up God in a coffee shop discussion, nobody is really offended. If I speak about Buddha or Brahman, Moses or Mohammed, I really don't irritate the listener. However, the name Jesus Christ seems to cut right to the soul. It did for me! When people brought up the other religious and philosophical leaders of history, I usually participated in some sort of intellectual discussion. When people tried to discuss Jesus with me, I felt that my space had been violated! What right did this person have to challenge me and my worldview? I've found that something makes Jesus more contentious and convicting than all the other religious leaders combined.

Really, what is it…?

Unlike any other widely followed religious leader in history, Jesus Christ made a unique claim. He declared himself God. Not a god, not god-like, but God incarnate—the creator of the universe in human flesh. Intellectually, that's very disturbing. Spiritually, that's a direct attack on everything comfortable and coexisting in my safe little world.

For me, I retreated to the typical responses to the life and claims of Jesus. Depending on the stage of my life, they sounded something like this:

"Jesus was a great man."

"Jesus was a nice moral model."

"Jesus was an esteemed teacher."

"Jesus was a religious prophet."

However, as Christian scholar Josh McDowell declares in his foundational book, *More than a Carpenter,* these types of statements raise a compelling "trilemma." Once you examine the actual claims of Jesus and his eyewitness followers, there are only three alternatives for who he really is—Jesus Christ was either a liar, a lunatic, or our Lord.

> *The issue with these three alternatives is not which is possible, for it is obvious that all three are possible. But rather, the question is 'which is more probable?' Who you decide Jesus Christ is must not be an idle intellectual exercise. You cannot put Him on the shelf as a great moral teacher. That is not a valid option. He is either a liar, a lunatic, or Lord and God. You must make a choice. 'But,' as the Apostle John wrote, 'these have been written that you may believe that Jesus is the Christ, the Son of God; and'—more important—'that believing you might have life in His name' (John 20:31).*[48]

C.S. Lewis, a popular British theologian, continues:

> *I am trying here to prevent anyone saying the really foolish thing that people often say about Him: 'I'm ready to accept Jesus as a great moral teacher, but I don't accept His claim to be God.' That is the one thing we must not say. A man who was merely a man and said the sort of things Jesus said would not be a great moral teacher. He would either be a lunatic—on the level with the man who says he is a poached egg—or else he would be the Devil of Hell. You must make your choice. Either this man was, and is, the Son of God: or else a madman or something worse. You can shut Him up for a fool, you can spit at Him and kill Him as a demon; or you can fall at His feet and call Him Lord and God. But let us not come with any patronising nonsense about His being a great human teacher. He has not left that open to us. He did not intend to.*[49]

Please understand, I'm not selling religion here. If anything, I still believe "religion" has kept more people from God than anything else in history.

---

48.   Josh McDowell, *More than a Carpenter,* Tyndale House Publishers, 1977, pp. 33-34.
49.   C.S. Lewis, *Mere Christianity,* The MacMillan Company, 1960, pp. 40-41.

Actually, I've discovered that true Christianity isn't a religion at all—it's discovering and establishing a relationship with God. It's trusting in Jesus and what He did on the cross for you and me,[50] not on what we can do for ourselves.[51]

True Christianity isn't about "organized religion." It's not about hierarchical structures, ornate buildings, flamboyant preachers, or traditional rules and rituals. In fact, let's just drop the "Christianity" label all together. Simply, it's pursuing and reconciling three basic questions of life:

1. **Does God exist?** If so, what am I going to do about it?

2. **Is the Bible true?** If so, what does that mean for me?

3. **Who is Jesus?** If he is who he claims to be, how will this reality change my life?

Again, it's not about religion at all…

It's not about the man-made machine we know today as "Christianity"…

It's all about Jesus.

He's either the Son of God who offers the only true hope for the world, or he's not.

Done.

---

50.   1 Corinthians 15:1-4—*Now, brothers, I want to remind you of the gospel I preached to you, which you received and on which you have taken your stand. By this gospel you are saved, if you hold firmly to the word I preached to you. Otherwise, you have believed in vain. For what I received I passed on to you as of first importance: that Christ died for our sins according to the Scriptures, that he was buried, that he was raised on the third day according to the Scriptures.*

51.   Ephesians 2:8-9—*For it is by grace you have been saved, through faith—and this not from yourselves, it is the gift of God—not by works, so that no one can boast.*

NOW WHAT...?

Why did I write this book and share it with you...?

...Because I went on an incredible, life-changing journey and I'm excited about that!

I hit a season in my life where I started asking questions again...
I started challenging my own worldview...
I woke up from a long slumber and opened my eyes a little wider!

◆   ◆   ◆

My only hope is that you'll start some kind of journey in your life!

Ask some questions...
Explore some assumptions...
Examine some long-held preconceptions about life, purpose and meaning...

◆   ◆   ◆

If you were selected for a jury in a real trial, you would be asked to affirm up front that you haven't formed any preconceptions about the case. You would be required to vow that you would be open-minded and fair, drawing your conclusions based on the weight of the facts and not your whims or prejudices. You would be urged to thoughtfully consider the credibility of the witnesses, carefully sift the testimony, and rigorously subject the evidence to your common sense and logic.

Ultimately it's the responsibility of jurors to reach a verdict. That doesn't mean they have one-hundred-percent certainty, because we can't have absolute proof about anything in life. In a trial, jurors are asked to weigh the evidence and come to the best possible conclusion.[52]

---

52. Strobel, *The Case for Christ*, 18.

◆   ◆   ◆

In no way do I think your journey has to mirror mine…

My only hope and prayer is that you'll start an honest quest…

FURTHER STUDY SUGGESTIONS—PART III

Lee Strobel, ***The Case for Christ***, Zondervan, 1998.
A journalist's personal investigation of the evidence for Jesus. Strobel, former legal editor at the Chicago Tribune, took a spiritual journey from atheism to faith by "cross-examining" a dozen recognized authorities in their fields.

Mark Eastman & Chuck Smith, ***The Search for Messiah***, TWFT/Joy Publishing, 1996.
Examine the powerful evidence from the Dead Sea Scrolls, as well as the beliefs of the ancient Jewish rabbis in connection with the identity of the Messiah.

Craig Blomberg, ***The Historical Reliability of the Gospels***, Intervarsity Press, 1987.
Is skepticism of the biblical text warranted or can we trust the New Testament to give us accurate historical information about Jesus? The current state of Gospel research and textual criticism.

Frank Morrison, ***Who Moved the Stone?*** Zondervan Publishing, reprint ed. 1958.
A classic apologetic on the resurrection. Morrison set out to disprove the resurrection as a myth and discovered the validity of the biblical record.

Randall Price, ***Secrets of the Dead Sea Scrolls***, Harvest House Publishers, 1996.
An easy-to-read, yet authoritative resource on the scrolls and their impact on biblical studies, textual criticism, and manuscript reliability.

Josh McDowell, ***More than a Carpenter***, Tyndale House Publishers, 1973.
Josh McDowell was another guy who thought Christians must be "out of their minds." As he put Christians down and argued against their faith, he discovered that his arguments weren't standing up against scrutiny. This book is simple and straight-forward for the skeptic.

John Foxe, ***Foxe's Book of Martyrs***, Baker Book House, W. Grinton Berry, editor, 2001 reprint.
The classic book that records the history of Christian persecution, torture and martyred deaths. The accounts of men and women who accepted death rather than deny the truth.

Gary Habermas, ***The Historical Jesus***, College Press Publishing, 1996.
Ancient evidence for the life of Jesus. Dr. Habermas combines his expertise as a philos-opher and historian to offer a careful analysis of current trends in the study of Jesus. He gives a balanced argument for the historicity of the New Testament documents and the evidence for the life, ministry, death and resurrection of Jesus of Nazareth.

Simon Greenleaf, ***The Testimony of the Evangelists***, Kregel Classics, 1995 reprint.
The Gospels examined by the Rules of Evidence. A classic study of the rules of evidence as applied to the New Testament accounts of the life of Jesus.

Is Jesus God? Website with Links: http://www.allaboutgod.com/is-jesus-god.htm

ABOUT THE AUTHOR

Randall Niles is a corporate attorney who's spent the last few years starting organizations dedicated to critical thinking and truth seeking. He's currently teaching college courses in the areas of business, law and philosophy. Randall's education includes Georgetown, Oxford and Berkeley. He lives in Colorado with his wife and three kids.

Requests for information should be addressed to:

Randall C. Niles
ThinkWorks™
7150 Campus Drive, Suite 320
Colorado Springs, CO 80920
Randall@Think-Works.com

0-595-32971-3

Printed in the United States
23037LVS00006B/118-510

9 780595 329717